Gem &
POCKET GUIDE

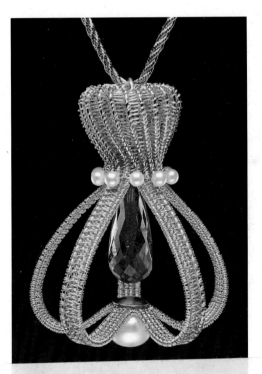

Gem & Jewelry
POCKET GUIDE

A traveler's guide to buying diamonds,
colored gems, pearls, gold and
platinum jewelry

Text & Photographs by
Renée Newman

except where otherwise indicated

International Jewelry Publications
Los Angeles _____

This publication is designed to provide information in regard to the subject matter covered. It is sold with the understanding that the publisher and author are not engaged in rendering legal, financial, or other professional services. If legal or other expert assistance is required, the services of a competent professional should be sought. International Jewelry Publications and the author shall have neither liability nor responsibility to any person or entity with respect to any loss or damage caused or alleged to be caused directly or indirectly by the information contained in this book. All inquiries should be directed to:

International Jewelry Publications
P.O. Box 13384
Los Angeles, CA 90013-0384 USA

(Include a self-addressed, stamped envelope with inquiry).

Printed in Singapore

Library of Congress Cataloging in Publication Data

Newman, Renée,
      Gem & jewelry pocket guide: a traveler's guide to buying diamonds, colored gems, pearls, gold and platinum jewelry / text & photographs by Renée Newman.
            p. cm.
      Includes bibliographical references and index.
      ISBN 0-929975-30-8
      1. Jewelry--Purchasing. 2. Precious stones--Purchasing 3. Diamonds--Purchasing. I. Title: Gem and jewelry pocket guide. II. Title.
TS 756.N49 2001
739.27'029'6--dc21   00-057518
      N 554 G

Cover photo: jewelry and gems from Cynthia Renée Co.; photo by John Parrish. Cover background photo by Dean Lange.
Title page: Pearls from King's Ransom; photo by Ron Fortier.
Photo of Tahiti facing title page by Dean Lange.

Contents

Acknowledgments

I'd like to express my appreciation to the following people for their contribution to the *Gem & Jewelry Pocket Guide*:

Dean & Lois Lange. They gave me the idea of writing a pocket guide for travelers.

Ernie and Regina Goldberger of the Josam Diamond Trading Corporation. This book could never have been written without the experience and knowledge I gained from working with them.

Eve Alfillé, C. R. Beesley, Michael Fleming, Pete Flusser, Josh Hall, Richard Hughes, James Joliff, Don Kay, Doug Kato, Dean & Lois Lange, Beryl Kirk, Jurgen Maerz, Sindi Schloss, Kathrin Schoenke, Robert Shapiro, and John White. They've made valuable suggestions, corrections and comments regarding the portions of the book they examined.

A.G.L., A & Z Pearls, A.I.G.S., Barbara Berk, Cynthia Renée Co., Divina Pearls, Extreme Gioielli, Gary Dulac Goldsmith, Richard Kimball, King's Ransom, Joe Landau, Glenn Lehrer Designs, Mason-Kay, Fred Mouawad, Murphy Design, Neshama, P.G.I., Port Royal Antique Jewelry, Linda Quinn, Robert Shapiro, The Roxx Limited, Varna Platinum, and Harry Winston Inc. Photos or diagrams from them have been reproduced in this book.

Carrie G Fine Gems, Peggy Croft, Ernie & Regina Goldberger, Mark Gronlund, King Plutarco, Danny & Ronny Levy, Overland Gems, Andrew Sarosi, Timeless Gem Designs, Varna Platinum. Their stones or jewelry have been used for some of the photos.

Greg Hatfield, Ion & Amy Itescu and Donald Nelson. They have provided technical assistance.

Louise Harris Berlin, the editor. Thanks to her, this book is easier for consumers to read and understand.

My sincere thanks to all of these contributors for their kind help.

Preface

Before becoming a gemologist, I was a full-time professional tour director. It was my exposure to gems in Asia, South America and the South Pacific that prompted me to take courses at the Gemological Institute of America and eventually pursue a full-time career as a gemologist.

Two of my former passengers, Dean and Lois Lange, suggested I write a condensed gem buying guide for travelers. They liked my other books, but found them too large and heavy to carry on trips. They wanted a pocket-size book with simple buying tips on all gems. I believe their wishes are representative of other travelers and shoppers, so I've written this book.

It contains highlights from my books on diamonds, pearls, colored gemstones and gold & platinum jewelry, but it also has additional information. Here's how the *Gem & Jewelry Pocket Guide* differs from my other books:

♦ The discussion of gem and jewelry evaluation is more concise.
♦ It contains a chapter on notable gem sources, which enables you to find quickly which countries are noted for specific gems.
♦ It includes information on amber, coral and ivory.
♦ There are two chapters on choosing jewelers and appraisers.
♦ Sample gem lab documents are included.
♦ It describes customs regulations, duties and websites.
♦ It outlines precautions you should take when buying jewelry abroad from someone you don't know.

The *Gem & Jewelry Pocket Guide* provides a concise overview of gems, gold and platinum; but if you're making a major purchase or if you're in the gem trade, read my other books too. When you go shopping, take this book along to assist you when buying gems and jewelry.

1

Colored Stone Price Factors in a Nutshell

The following factors can affect the prices of colored gemstones:

♦ **Color**
♦ **Cut quality** (proportions and finish)
♦ **Stone shape and cutting style**
♦ **Carat weight or stone size**
♦ **Clarity** (degree to which a stone is free from flaws)
♦ **Transparency**
♦ **Treatment status** (untreated or treated? type and extent of the treatment)
♦ **Distinctness of phenomena** if present (e.g., stars, cat's-eyes, alexandrite's change of color, opal's play of color)

The pricing of colored gems is also determined by market factors such as demand, form of payment, buyer's credit rating, amount purchased and competitors' prices. Often you can find the same dealer selling a stone of higher quality for less than one of lower quality. This is because the rough for the higher quality stone may have cost less. Or, the rate of currency exchange could have been more favorable at the time of purchase. Therefore, you should not assume that higher price necessarily means higher quality. Conversely, lower price is not necessarily indicative of a deal.

Why the 4 C's is Not an Adequate Pricing System

You may be surprised that there are more than four price factors if you've heard about the 4 C's of color, cut, clarity and carat weight. The 4 C's system of valuing gems is a clever, convenient way to explain gem pricing. The problem is that it causes consumers to overlook the importance of cut quality, transparency and treatment status.

If you see a mini gem-lab report stating that the shape/cut of a gemstone is round brilliant, you may assume that this tells you everything about the cut of stone when in fact it doesn't. The quality of the cut is important and it's a separate price factor from shape and cutting style.

If you're not informed about gem treatments, you may assume, for example, that two equally attractive jade stones should be priced alike. However, if one is dyed or bleached and the other is of natural color, their prices should be quite different. Chapter 2 describes the various ways in which gems are treated.

If you're comparing a cloudy stone to a transparent one, be aware that transparency can have a significant impact on their value. Transparency and clarity are often interconnected, but they're not the same. A stone can be transparent like crystal yet have a low clarity. Likewise a stone may be flawless, yet be cloudy and milky in appearance.

Price Factors Explained

COLOR: It can be broken into three components:

Hue: Colors like those in a rainbow such as blue, green and bluish green. Brown, black, gray & white are not considered to be hues.

Tone: The amount of color, the degree of lightness or darkness

Amount of grey or brown masking the hue: This component is called different names such as "saturation," "intensity," and "color mask" depending upon the color system you're using. Stones with a high color saturation, for example, have hardly any grey or brown masking the hue.

Gem dealers often disagree on what is the best hue and tone for a given gemstone such as sapphire or emerald. They agree, however, that for most gem varieties, the less brown or gray that is present, the more valuable the stone. For example, the center ruby in figure 1.1 is worth a lot more than the brownish rubies on each side.

If you're buying a gemstone for yourself, it doesn't matter what color you choose as long as you like it and the color looks

Fig. 1.1 A ruby with good red color flanked by two rubies which have a much less valuable color—brownish red.

good on you. However, when buying gems for resale or as gifts, find out what hues and tones gem dealers prefer. Chapter Four describes the preferred colors for various gem varieties. Usually the strongest and richest colors are the most valuable. Very light and very dark stones typically cost less.

When judging color:

♦ Clean the gemstone with a soft cloth if it's dirty.

♦ Rotate the stone and examine it from various angles, keeping in mind, however, that color is judged in the face-up position.

♦ Look at the stone under different types of light such as an incandescent light-bulb, fluorescent light and daylight. Top quality stones look good under all types of light. Daylight equivalent light is the standard used for gem grading.

♦ Examine the stone against a variety of backgrounds—white, black and against your skin.

♦ Look at the stone under direct light and away from it. Good quality gemstones are also colorful out of direct light.

♦ Examine the stone for color zoning—the uneven distribution of color. When the color is uneven or concentrated in one spot, this can sometimes decrease the stone's value. Obvious color zoning is most serious when visible in the face-up view of a stone.

♦ Compare the stone side by side with other stones of the same variety. Color nuances will be more apparent.

Fig. 1.2 Tanzanite without a window   **Fig. 1.3** Tanzanite with a window

♦ **CUT QUALITY**: A well-cut gemstone displays brilliance and color throughout the stone (fig 1.2). It shouldn't have an obvious **window**—a pale, washed out area in the middle of the stone that allows you to see right through it (fig. 1.3). In general, the larger the window, the poorer the cut.

To look for windows, hold the stone about an inch or two (2–5 cm) above a contrasting background such as your hand or a printed page. Then try to look straight through the top of the stone without tilting it. The stone has a window if you can see your hand, the print or the background through the center of it.

When buying a gemstone, be sure to look at its profile. The side view will show you if the stone is too deep for the mounting, too shallow or too bulky. Diagram 1.1 shows you the profile of a well-cut colored gemstone and defines terminology related to gemstone cut. Figure 1.4 is another example.

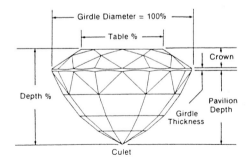

Diagram 1.1 Profile of a mixed-cut colored gemstone.
Copyright 1978 by American Gemological Laboratories.

. 1.4 A well-cut tanzanite. Do
expect rubies and emeralds
·e this well-proportioned.

Fig. 1.5 Tanzanite with a crown that is too
high, a pavilion that is too shallow and a
girdle that's too thick.

Figure 1.5 illustrates a poorly proportioned tanzanite. This
stone was cut to maximize weight from the rough at the expense
of beauty. The shallow pavilion (bottom) reduces brilliance and
creates a large window. The high crown (top) and thick girdle
(rim around stone) add unnecessary weight, which increases the
price of the stone. Faceted gems are usually priced by weight.

When judging cut, consider, too, the quality, complexity and
originality of the faceting (arrangement of small polished surfaces
called facets). Some of the best faceting is done on low- and
medium-priced gem material such as aquamarine, garnet, quartz,
tanzanite, topaz and tourmaline. The faceting and proportioning
of more expensive gems like emeralds, rubies and alexandrites is
often less precise because the higher cost of the rough leads many
cutters to be more interested in retaining weight than in maximiz-
ing beauty. For a fuller discussion of cut evaluation, consult the
Gemstone Buying Guide or *Ruby, Sapphire & Emerald Buying
Guide* by Renée Newman.

SHAPE & CUTTING STYLE: A gem's **shape** is its face-up
outline. The most common gemstone shapes include the round,
oval, square, triangle, pear, marquise, heart and **cushion**, a
squarish or rectangular shape with curved sides and rounded
corners. Gems can be any geometric shape or they may resemble

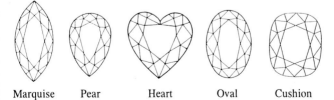

Marquise   Pear   Heart   Oval   Cushion

objects such as animals, bells, stars, the moon, etc. They can also be cut as abstract freeforms. Gem cutters try to select shapes and cutting styles which allow them to emphasize preferred colors and brilliance, minimize undesirable flaws, and/or get the maximum weight yield from the rough. In small calibrated sizes, there is a tendency to cut what jewelry manufacturers want, even when some shapes cause a greater weight loss. Standard sizes and shapes are required for mass-produced jewelry.

The effect of shape on price varies depending on the seller, the gem variety, the stone weight, the stone quality and the demand for the shape. A high-quality, one-carat round ruby, for example, may cost 15% to 20% more than one with a cushion shape. In small sizes and low qualities, the shape may have no effect on the price. The subject of shape pricing is too complicated for this book. Simply remember to compare gemstones of the same shape and cutting style when evaluating gem prices.

Cutting style refers to the way in which a stone is cut or faceted. An oval-shaped stone, for example, may just be rounded as a **cabochon** (stone with a dome-shaped top and either a flat or rounded bottom) or it may have **facets** (polished surfaces with varying shapes) that are arranged in different styles.

There are three traditional faceting styles:

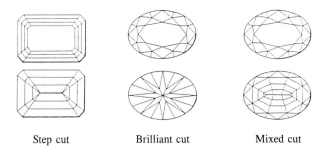

Step cut   Brilliant cut   Mixed cut

Step cut: Has rows of facets that resemble the steps of a staircase. The facets are usually four-sided and elongated, and parallel to the girdle. If step-cuts have clipped-off corners creating an octagonal shape, they're called **emerald cuts** because emeralds

octagonal shape, they're called **emerald cuts** because emeralds are often cut this way.

Brilliant cut: Has mostly 3-sided facets which radiate outward. Kite- or lozenge-shaped facets may also be present.

Mixed cut: Has both step- and brilliant-cut facets. This is a popular faceting style for colored stones.

Many new faceting styles have appeared on the market and gemstones are also carved. Well-proportioned, designer cuts typically cost more than traditional cuts. The cabochon is the lowest priced cutting style.

Cabochon

CARAT WEIGHT OR STONE SIZE: A **carat** is a unit of weight equalling a fifth of a gram. In most cases, the higher the carat weight category, the greater the per-carat price. However, a one-carat ruby, for example, is worth far more than several small rubies of similar quality with a total weight of one carat. This is because the supply of large rubies is more limited. So when you compare jewelry prices, besides noting the quality, you should pay attention to individual stone weights and notice the difference between the labels **1 ct TW** (one carat total weight) and **1 ct** (the weight of one stone).

When comparing the cost of transparent gems, you should also note the **per-carat cost** instead of concentrating on the total cost of the stone. This makes it easier to compare prices more accurately, which is why dealers buy and sell most gems using per-carat prices. The following equations will help you calculate the per-carat cost and total cost of gemstones.

Per-carat cost = stone cost ÷ carat weight

Total cost of a stone = carat weight × per-carat cost

Many translucent to opaque stones such as jade, malachite and chalcedony are sold by the piece or stone size, not by weight. Designer cuts may also be priced per piece, and colored stones under about a half of a carat are often priced according to millimeter size.

Fig. 1.6 A high-clarity tanzanite

Fig. 1.7 A low-clarity tanzanite

CLARITY: Clarity is the degree to which a stone is free from flaws (clarity features). Flaws inside the stone (e.g., cracks, crystals, fluid-filled spaces) are called **inclusions.** Flaws on a stone's surface (e.g., scratches, pits, abrasions) are **blemishes.** When gems have no eye-visible flaws, they're said to be **eye clean**.

Some gems are more likely to have inclusions than others. Emeralds, for example, typically have some eye-visible flaws. Aquamarine, on the other hand, is normally eye clean. As a result, there is a greater tolerance for noticeable inclusions in emerald than in aquamarine. Two other gems that usually have eye-visible flaws are ruby and alexandrite. Some stones that normally have a high clarity like aquamarine are blue zircon, citrine, green tourmaline, kunzite, topaz and tanzanite. Some colored gems that fall between these high- and low-clarity groups include amethyst, blue tourmaline, garnet, iolite, peridot, sapphire, spinel and zircon that is green, orange or red.

Since clarity can vary from one gem variety to another, compare stones of the same type when judging clarity. The higher the clarity, the more valuable the gemstone. Judge clarity first with the naked eye. Then use a 10-power magnifier to help you spot inclusions such as cracks, which create durability problems. Magnification may also help you detect dye and other treatments.

Although clarity grading systems have been developed for colored stones, there's no one standardized system. Even when a single system is used, there can be a wide variation in how grades are assigned by appraisers. Therefore, it's best for you to ask appraisers and jewelers what their clarity grades mean when they use grades.

TRANSPARENCY: Gemstones that look cloudy or translucent have finely divided particles that interrupt the passage of light. Some gem laboratories refer to these fine particles as **texture**. Large particles may also create texture and diminish the transparency of a gemstone. The presence of a lot of texture also affects the color, making it look more grayish and dull.

Transparency can have a major impact on the value of a gemstone, especially on emerald, ruby, sapphire, opal, jade, star gems and cat's-eye gems. For example, a $20 Indian star ruby that's nearly opaque could possibly sell for as much as $400 if it were translucent or semi-transparent. (An opaque material does not allow light to pass through it; a translucent material resembles frosted glass.) A $10 sapphire that's nearly opaque could possibly sell for hundreds of dollars if it were transparent.

Normally the higher the transparency the more valuable the stone. There are a couple exceptions. Rubies and sapphires with a **slight** amount of texture, which disperses the color, may be valued the same or sometimes a bit more than stones with a diamond-like transparency. For black opal, opaque stones tend to be more highly valued than those with a higher transparency.

Fig. 1.8 Emerald with a high transparency and noticeable flaws

Fig. 1.9 Less transparent emerald than the one in figure 1.8

TREATMENT STATUS: Most colored stones are treated in some way to improve their color, clarity and/or brilliance. High quality untreated gems are usually the most highly valued. Not all treat-

Fig. 1.10 An early 20th century black opal ring. The play of color and intensity of the red is exceptional. Opals of this quality have sold for over $15,000 per carat. *Ring from Port Royal Antique Jewelry; photo by Harold & Erica Van Pelt.*

ments are equal. Some treatments such as dyeing and fracture filling have a more negative impact on value than others such as heat treatment. The next chapter discusses the various types of gem treatments.

DISTINCTNESS OF PHENOMENA: Phenomena are unusual optical effects. For example, some gem varieties such as ruby, sapphire, garnet, spinel and rose quartz may show a star effect. A cat's-eye effect may be seen on some quartz, emerald, aquamarine, chrysoberyl and tourmaline. The sharper and more obvious the star or cat's-eye, the more valuable the stone, all other factors being equal. However, don't expect the phenomena of natural stones to be as distinct as those on man-made stones.

Fig. 1.11 A cracked opal with little play of color, which cost $5

Gems display other kinds of phenomena too, but the most familiar type is the play of color found in opal. See the section on opal for more information about evaluating play of color. In general, the more prominent the phenomenal effect the more valuable the gem.

2

Treatments

If the supply of gems were limited to those specimens that are naturally attractive, they'd be so expensive that most of us could never own them. Therefore, many gems are treated. A **treatment** is any process such as heating, oiling, irradiation, waxing, or dying which alters the appearance of a gem.

Gem Treatments

HEAT TREATMENT: For centuries, gems have been heated to improve their color. However, in the past 30 years, heat treatment has been conducted on a wider scale and at much higher temperatures—1600°C (2900°F) and above. Besides lightening or darkening the color of a stone, heat can improve its clarity. Unless a receipt or lab document states otherwise, assume that the following gemstones have probably been heat-treated: aquamarine, carnelian, citrine, ruby, sapphire, tanzanite, pink topaz, blue and red zircon, and green tourmaline. The color is usually stable.

HPHT TREATMENT (High pressure, high heat treatment): This is a new diamond treatment. It's used to turn a special class of brown diamonds colorless or greenish yellow. The color is stable.

IRRADIATION: Only certain gem varieties can be enhanced with irradiation. They include:

"Black" or dark-color pearls: from off-color bleached pearls; stable, after a slight fading just after treatment.

Blue topaz: from colorless topaz; irradiation turns it brown and then heat treatment makes it a stable blue color.

Diamonds that are green, blue, yellow or brown: from light yellow or brown diamond; stable.

Smoky quartz: from colorless quartz (rock crystal); stable.

Fig. 2.1 Typical color of rough Sri Lankan sapphire prior to heat treatment. *Photo by C. R. Beesley of AGL.*

Fig. 2.2 Results of heating sapphire figure 2.1. *Photo by C. R. Beesley*

Pink and red tourmaline: from light pink tourmaline; relatively stable, but strong heat from lights, for example, may sometimes cause it to fade.

Yellow beryl: from colorless beryl; some fades in light or heat.

Yellow or orange sapphire: from colorless and light yellow sapphire; fades quickly. Most yellow sapphire is heat treated.

BLEACHING: Chemicals may be used to lighten or remove color. Pearls, coral and ivory are commonly bleached. Jadeite is often bleached and then impregnated with a synthetic material.

FRACTURE & CAVITY FILLING: If surface fractures in gems are filled with an appropriate substance, the fractures are less noticeable and the overall color and transparency may improve. Oil, wax, glass, resins or epoxy-like substances are used as fillers. Some fillings can evaporate over time and leave a white or brown residue. Most fillers are affected by the heat of a jeweler's torch.

Almost all emeralds are fracture-filled with oil, wax, resins or epoxy like substances. Some diamonds are fracture-filled with a glass-like film. Rubies may have oil, epoxy or glass fillings, and the fillings may be in fractures or cavities. Unfilled stones are preferred over filled ones. The less filling present the better the stone. Fracture fillings are more stable than cavity fillings.

DYEING: Rubies, emeralds, jade and other stones that may have small surface cracks are occasionally dyed with colored oils, epoxies or dyes, especially if they're of low quality. Some gemstones like lapis lazuli, chalcedony and agate don't need surface cracks to accept dye. They are naturally porous and often dyed. Black onyx is just dyed chalcedony. Pearls and matrix opal may also be dyed.

SURFACE DIFFUSION: This treatment can produce ruby, green topaz or blue, yellow and orange sapphire from pale or gray stones, or it can cause a star to form. The pale stones are packed in chemical powders which impart color and then heated to 1700°C and above until a thin layer of color covers their surface. The color is permanent, but remains only on the surface of the stone. Consequently, the color can be polished or scraped off, leaving the grey or white interior exposed.

IMPREGNATION and COATING with wax or plastic: Gems are waxed and plasticized to hide cracks and to make the surface look shiny. Impregnation can also improve durability and color. Some of the stones undergoing this treatment are turquoise, jade, lapis, malachite, emerald and amazonite. Other coating materials include lacquer, enamel, diamond film and ink.

LASER DRILLING: This treatment is done to get rid of dark "flaws" (inclusions) in diamonds. A focused laser beam is used to drill a narrow hole to the dark area in the diamond. If the inclusion is not vaporized by the laser itself, then it's dissolved or bleached with acid. After the treatment, the hole looks like a white dot face-up and like a thin white line from the side-view, except if it's been glass filled to help conceal the line.

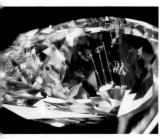 

. **2.3** Laser drill holes in a diamond   **Fig. 2.4** Same diamond viewed face-up

Not all gemstones are treated. Alexandrite, ametrine, garnet, iolite, moonstone and spinel are normally untreated.

Why Some Treatments are More Accepted than Others

Not all treatments are regarded as equal. Consider these factors when determining the acceptability of a treated gemstone:

♦ Is the treatment permanent?
♦ Has the treatment added foreign material to the gemstone?
♦ Has the internal character of the gemstone been changed by the treatment?.
♦ Does the treatment decrease durability?
♦ Does the treated gem compete with a natural gem?
♦ How available are attractive untreated gems of the same type?

PERMANENCE: Irradiated yellow sapphires may fade within minutes of being treated so they're not accepted. However, the heat treatment of sapphires is accepted because a stable color is usually produced.

The color of irradiated pearls is stable and does not rub off on your skin like the dye of some dyed pearls. This is one reason irradiated pearls are preferred over dyed pearls.

Laser drilling is a more accepted diamond treatment than fracture filling because lasering produces permanent results. Fracture filling is subject to change if the filled diamonds come in contact with a jewelers' torch or if they're subjected to prolonged or multiple ultrasonic cleanings. Some fillings cloud or discolor when exposed to light for long periods.

ADDITION OF FOREIGN MATERIAL: Another reason why heating and irradiation may be preferred to other treatments is that no chemicals, oils, wax or synthetic substances are added to the stones, except when the stones are heated in borax. When the borax turns into glass and fills cracks or cavities, this is undesirable and can reduce the value of expensive rubies, for example.

INTERNAL CHANGE: Heat treatment done at 1600°C (2900°F) and above can melt inclusions, create tiny stress cracks, produce a hazy appearance and change the overall internal character of a gemstone. This is one reason why low-temperature heat treatment is preferred to high temperature heating.

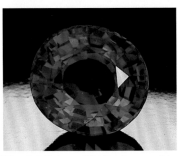

2.5 Abraded facet edges of a new y that was improperly heat treated

Fig. 2.6 Unheated Sri Lankan sapphire (15.25 cts). *Photo from Fred Mouawad.*

DURABILITY: Treatments can have a negative effect on durability. Dr. Kurt Nassau writes in his book, *Gemstone Enhancement* (pg.43), "High temperature heat treatments may cause some materials to become more brittle and show more wear."

The *GIA Gem Reference Guide* notes on page 262 in the section on zircon, "Toughness: heat-treated stones—poor to fair; untreated stones—fair to good."

According to Dr. Horst Krupp, a heat treater and physicist, high temperature heat treatment can cause rubies and sapphires to become brittle and abrade if they're not properly cooled during the heat treatment process (personal communication). This is another reason high temperature heating can have a negative impact on gem prices.

Burmese jade is sometimes soaked and bleached in chemicals to remove brown or yellow impurities. This weakens the jade. Occasionally treatments can improve durability. Most natural turquoise can crack or crumble. When it's impregnated with a plastic material, it becomes more durable.

COMPETITION: Small Japanese pearls (akoya pearls) that have been darkened by irradiation and/or dyes are accepted by the trade because the treatments provide consumers with an option not available from natural-color akoya pearls.

Artificially colored South Sea pearls are not well accepted. In fact they're banned in Tahiti because they compete with Tahiti's naturally colored black pearls, and they confuse buyers.

There are strong objections to the new HPHT-treated diamonds because they compete with high-quality untreated diamonds and they complicate buying, selling and identification.

Most tanzanite is heat-treated to intensify the color and/or eliminate brown, gray or green. The low-temperature heat treatment (600-700 degrees centigrade), which produces a stable color, is well accepted and is used even on the finest stones. Tanzanite was unknown before the 1960's, so heat treated tanzanite has not competed with an existing market of untreated stones. Contrary to what is sometimes reported, there are attractive untreated tanzanites, but the percentage is negligible.

AVAILABILITY; Oiling emeralds is a well-accepted trade practice because emeralds typically have cracks and need to be fracture filled to improve their clarity. Therefore when buying expensive emeralds, assume they've been fracture-filled with oil or some other substance. Your main concern should be to what extent has the treatment affected the appearance. This information is now provided on many emerald lab reports.

Unoiled rubies are readily available, so ruby oiling isn't accepted even though it's often done when surface cracks are present.

Precautions to Take When Buying Expensive Gems

When you spend a few hundred dollars on a gem, the treatment status is normally not a major issue. In fact, you can just assume that the rubies, sapphires, aquamarines and tanzanites you see have been heat treated and the emeralds have been fracture filled. Enjoy wearing these gems and appreciate that fact that treatments allow you to buy more attractive stones at lower prices.

However, when you spend a few thousand dollars or more on a gemstone, the type and extent of the treatment is an important buying factor. Take these precautions:

♦ Deal with sellers who can explain treatments in frank simple language rather than with euphemisms and vague terms.
♦ Deal with sellers who will tell you both the bad and good points about treatments.
♦ Ask if and how stones have been treated. The answer will give you insight into the seller's ethics.
♦ Have the salesperson include treatment information on the receipt. If the stone is untreated, have this written.
♦ For expensive gems, get a report from a lab that automatically includes treatment information on their documents.

3

Synthetic and Imitation Gems

A natural gemstone comes from the ground and is a product of nature, not of man.

The word **synthetic** is used to describe a gemstone made in a lab that has the same basic chemical composition as its natural counterpart. For example, synthetic ruby has the same chemical composition as natural ruby. It also has similar chemical, optical and physical properties.

Imitations, on the other hand, do not have the same chemical composition as the stones they resemble, and they may be made by nature or by man. Red glass, for example, can be a man-made imitation of ruby. Garnets used to mimic rubies would be natural imitations.

Fig. 3.1 Synthetic sapphire. *Ring and photo from Varna Platinum.*

Since consumers tend to interpret the word "synthetic" differently than jewelers, people who sell synthetic stones usually prefer to describe them with terms such as **created**, **lab-grown** or **man-made**. Gemologists and natural stone dealers usually identify lab-grown stones as synthetic stones.

Cultured is sometimes used incorrectly as a synonym for "lab-grown." The two terms, however, are not equivalent. Culturing pearls is a more natural process than growing gems.

Synthetic gems are not just a recent phenomenon. Lab-grown ruby, the first synthetic, has been sold commercially since the early 1900's; if your grandmother has some ruby jewelry, the stones could very well have been made in a laboratory. Today, lab-grown stones are even more common, especially in birthstone jewelry and class rings. Synthetic stones are also found in designer jewelry (fig. 3.1), set with diamonds in gold or platinum. Some of the stones that are synthetically produced and sold to consumers in jewelry are:

Synthetic alexandrite	Synthetic opal
Synthetic amethyst	Synthetic ruby
Synthetic chrysoberyl	Synthetic sapphire
Synthetic diamond	Synthetic spinel
Synthetic emerald	Synthetic turquoise

Some stores call imitation stones "synthetic." For example, imitation tanzanite may be sold as "synthetic tanzanite" because "synthetic" sounds better than "imitation." Green CZ (cubic zirconia) is often called synthetic emerald. Green CZ is a lab-grown stone, but it's not synthetic emerald. It's synthetic CZ, which is much cheaper than lab-grown emerald.

In most countries, it's against the law to call a synthetic ruby, for example, simply a ruby. Not all countries, however, have laws like this and some stores don't follow the law. Therefore when buying expensive gems abroad, have the store specify on the receipt if the stone is of natural origin. This is added protection for you. Technically synthetic ruby is ruby. Ethically, though, it should be called synthetic or lab-grown ruby.

Deceptive Practices:

Listed below are practices that are normally done with the intent to deceive. All of them, however, can be considered legitimate when they're properly disclosed to buyers.

COATING WITH COLORED SUBSTANCES: Colorless or pale colored stones are sometimes coated with colored plastic. Green plastic coatings are used to make colorless beryl look like emerald and light green jade like valuable imperial jade. Occasionally, transparent metallic coatings, like those on camera lenses, are applied to colorless gems to add color or brilliance. Varnish and lacquer coatings may also be used.

PAINTING: You don't have to cover a pale stone with a colored coating to make it look colorful. A little paint in the right spot(s) can do the job. Because of the multiple reflections in a faceted transparent gem, a dab or two of paint on the bottom and/or edge of the stone can make it appear evenly colored when viewed face up. The paint can be hidden by the mounting.

Emeralds have at times been colored in this manner. Translucent opal cabochons may be painted on the bottom to enhance and intensify their play of color. Peacock feathers, multicolored butterfly wings and mother of pearl have on occasion been placed behind opal to improve color play too. Sometimes purple ink is applied on the back of yellowish diamonds or under the prongs of the setting to make the diamonds appear almost colorless and more valuable. Since purple is the complimentary color of yellow, it has the effect of absorbing part of the yellow color. As a result, **beware of closed-back settings**. The bottom of the stone may be painted.

FOIL BACKING: For centuries, foil backings have been used to add color and brilliance to gems. As gem-cutting techniques progressed and brought out more brilliance in stones, these backings became less popular. Today foil backings are occasionally found on genuine stones, but they're more likely to be seen on glass imitations. Again, **beware of closed-back settings**. Something such as foil may be concealed underneath the stones, particularly if they're unusually bright. Foil-backed stones are commonly found in antique pieces. The price of this jewelry should be based on its antique value.

QUENCH CRACKLING: Stones that are quench crackled have been heated and then plunged into cold water. This procedure is done to produce cracks in synthetic stones so they'll look more natural. Colorless quartz may be quench crackled so it can afterwards be fracture-filled with colored oil or dyes and used to imitate emerald or ruby.

MAKING COMPOSITE STONES (Assembled Stones): Stones formed from two or more parts are called **composite** or **assembled stones**. If they're composed of two parts, they're **doublets**. Those consisting of three parts are **triplets**. Assembled opals are one of the most typical composite stones. Opal doublets and triplets are

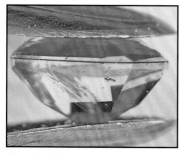

Fig. 3.2 Side view of a composite stone immersed in water. Note the dark green line around the girdle where the two parts are joined with green cement.

Fig. 3.3 Face up view of the sa: stone, which was made to look lik deep-green emerald.

normally disclosed and sold in a legitimate manner so selling them is **not** considered a deceptive practice. Ruby, sapphire, emerald and jade assembled stones, however, are generally used to trick buyers.

For example, pale yellow sapphire pieces may be cemented with a blue glue to form a blue sapphire. Two pieces of pale emerald may be joined together with a green gelatin or cement to make it appear like a deep green emerald (figs. 3.2 & 3.3).

Jade is sometimes made into triplets. They consist of pale jade that has been hollowed out, filled with a green gel and smaller cabochon and then cemented to a jade back to make it look like expensive green jade.

The key to identifying a composite stone is to find where its parts have been joined together. This can often be seen by immersing the stone in water (immersion tends to make color differences and the glue layer more obvious). However, don't immerse assembled opals in water or other liquids; just look at them from the side. Magnification is another helpful identifying technique. It can reveal separation lines, flattened air bubbles between the parts or swirly areas where the stone has been brushed with glue.

Beware of gem prices that seem to good to be true. The stone(s) could either be fake, assembled, coated or lab grown.

4

Colored Gemstones

Alexandrite & Cat's-eye (Chrysoberyl)

Alexandrite and cat's-eye look very different, yet they're the same mineral—chrysoberyl (kris´so berl´). A less expensive type of chrysoberyl, simply called chrysoberyl, is transparent, shows no optical effects and ranges in color from green, to yellow to brown.

ALEXANDRITE: Natural alexandrite is hard to find in jewelry stores. When you do see it for sale, the colors are likely to be a grayish green and brownish purple or lavender. In its finest qualities, though, alexandrite looks green in sunlight and purplish-red under incandescent light (light bulbs). Prices for natural alexandrites that show a noticeable change of color start at about $1500 per carat retail and can go over $20,000 per carat depending on size, quality, and the distinctness and type of color change.

g. 4.1 Russian alexandrite under candescent light. (The color of gems photos is usually somewhat different in their actual color.)

Fig. 4.2 Same stone as it appears in daylight. A color change as distinct as this is rare in alexandrite.

CAT'S-EYE: The unmodified term **cat's-eye** means chrysoberyl cat's-eye. Other minerals such as quartz, tourmaline and beryl may also display a cat's-eye (stripe of reflected light across a cabochon), but chrysoberyl cat's-eye is the most prized and has the sharpest eye. Other cat's-eye stones must indicate the mineral, as for example, cat's-eye quartz or quartz cat's-eye.

Fig. 4.3 Cat's-eye

A brownish yellow similar to the color of honey is the most valued color, but greenish-yellow stones can also be very expensive. In the finest qualities, cat's-eye can wholesale for over $3000 per carat. Stones with fuzzy, non-sharp eyes, dull colors and eye-visible inclusions can sell for less than $100 per carat. Cat's-eye can also display a color change. Alexandrite cat's-eyes, however, are quite rare.

Major sources: Brazil and Sri Lanka are the primary sources of chrysoberyls. Other deposits are in Russia, Tanzania, Zimbabwe, Madagascar and Myanmar..

Beware: There's a lot of synthetic and imitation alexandrite on the market. If an "alexandrite" is large and flawless, assume it's synthetic or fake. Natural alexandrite with a distinct color change tends to have many flaws. If a seller tells you a stone is natural, have him write "natural alexandrite" on the receipt.

Lower priced quartz cat's-eye is often sold as cat's-eye. Therefore verify that cat's-eyes are chrysoberyl, and have this written on the receipt.

Care tips: If chrysoberyl stones are **not** fractured or heavily flawed, it's safe to clean them in ultrasonics and steamers; otherwise they can be safely cleaned in soap and water. Chrysoberyl is stable to heat and light; it doesn't react to chemicals; it's hard, strong and generally very durable.

Amethyst & Other Quartz Gems

Because of their abundance, quartz gemstones are quite affordable. Amethyst, the most expensive variety, might retail from $2 to $100 per carat depending on quality, cut and size. Even amethysts that sell for $15 per carat can look good.

AMETHYST (Purple or violet quartz): The most expensive color is an intense, deep, evenly-colored purple with flashes of red under incandescent light. The least costly is pale lavender. Four major sources of amethyst are Brazil, Uruguay, Bolivia and Zambia. A lot of synthetic amethyst, citrine and other colors of synthetic quartz are made in Japan and especially in Russia. Some amethyst is heat-treated to lighten its color or to transform it into citrine and sometimes green quartz.

Fig. 4.4 Amethyst

AMETRINE (Purple and yellow quartz). This popular gem is mined commercially in Bolivia and has only been available since the late 1980's.

CITRINE (Yellow or orange quartz): Most citrine is heat-treated amethyst or smoky quartz. Natural-color citrine is rare and is usually pale yellow. Its name is derived from the French word for lemon—citron. A lot of citrine is sold as topaz.

DRUSY QUARTZ: A bed of tiny quartz crystals found in hollow rock cavities. Drusy quartz is sometimes used as a jewelry accent.

QUARTZ CAT'S-EYE: Sri-Lanka, India and Brazil are sources of quartz cat's-eye. It may be white, green, yellow or brown.

ROCK CRYSTAL (Colorless quartz): This is the most widely distributed variety of quartz.

ROSE QUARTZ (Pink quartz): This quartz, which is typically translucent, is sometimes irradiated to intensify its color.

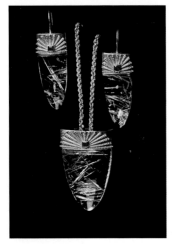

Fig. 4.5 Rutilated quartz. *Pendant and photo from Neshama.*

Fig. 4.6 A citrine, which was carved Mark Gronlund.

RUTILATED QUARTZ: Colorless transparent quartz that has needle-like inclusions of a mineral called rutile.

SMOKY QUARTZ (Brown to black quartz): Even though smoky quartz is found worldwide, some of it on the market is irradiated rock crystal and this tends to be very dark. This quartz is often sold incorrectly under the misnomer "smoky topaz."

TIGER'S-EYE: A translucent to opaque quartz with a silky luster and brown and gold stripes. Stones cut *en cabochon* with a gold band along the center resemble a cat's-eye. South Africa is the most important source of tiger's-eye. A grayish-blue quartz with a similar cat's-eye effect is called **HAWK'S-EYE**.

Care tips: Avoid strong heat because it may change the color of amethyst, citrine, rose quartz and smoky quartz. Some rose quartz and amethyst may fade in light.

In general, quartz is a fairly durable stone and can be safely cleaned in most ultrasonic cleaners if it's not fractured. It can also be safely washed in warm soapy water. Avoid steam cleaning and sudden temperature changes because they can cause fracturing or cleaving. Quartz reacts to hydrofluoric acid and alkalies.

Chalcedony

Chalcedony (kal sed´nee) is quartz that is composed of microscopic-size crystals. It's affordable, durable and suitable for fine carving. Members of the chalcedony species include:

AGATE: Dealers tend to apply the term agate to any patterned chalcedony that is translucent, as opposed to jasper which is usually opaque to the naked eye. In a more strict usage, agate is a chalcedony with curved or angular bands (layers) of color.

Certain types of colorless or gray agates from Brazil and Madagascar are often stained (permanently dyed) red, black, green, blue or yellow. with stable, inorganic chemicals. The main cutting and processing center for agate is Idar-0berstein in Germany, where a lot of agate used to be mined. Now it's shipped there from Brazil and Madagascar. Other sources of agate are Uruguay, Mexico, the U.S., Russia and India.

Some white, gray or colorless chalcedony with inclusions is called agate. **MOSS AGATE** has moss-like green, brown, and/or red inclusions. **DENDRITIC AGATE (LANDSCAPE AGATE)** has dark inclusions that resemble trees or ferns.

BLOODSTONE: An opaque dark green chalcedony with orange or red spots, which some Christians thought represented the blood of Jesus Christ. India is the main source of bloodstone.

CARNELIAN: Translucent orange or red chalcedony. Essentially all material sold as carnelian is heat-treated or stained and heat-treated chalcedony.

CHALCEDONY: White, gray or bluish gray chalcedony. Some of the main deposits are in Brazil, Madagascar, India and the United States.

BLUE CHALCEDONY: This is the most prized chalcedony, with the possible exception of fine inclusion specimens. Blue material from Namibia and other localities is currently very popular and usually sells by carat weight.

CHRYSOPRASE: Translucent light- to medium-green chalcedony, somewhat resembling jade. It used to be the most prized chalcedony

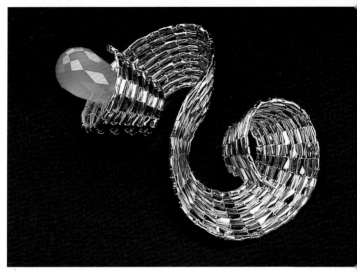

Fig. 4.7 Blue chalcedony. *Platinum brooch by Barbara Berk; photo by Dana Da*

Fig. 4.8 Hand carved carnelian drusy agate. *18K rose gold pendant/pin crea and photographed by Glenn Lehrer.*

variety. Since 1965, the best quality chrysoprase has come from Queensland, and more recently Western Australia. Other sources are Brazil, Poland and Kazakstan.

FIRE AGATE: A stone that displays an iridescent layer of thin iron oxide crystals under transparent chalcedony when it's cut and polished. You're most likely to find it for sale in Arizona, New Mexico and Mexico, the areas where fire agate is mined.

JASPER: An opaque, fine-grained chalcedony. It's usually multicolored, spotted or striped but can be uniformly colored. The most common colors are red, brown, yellow, gray and green. Blue and black are more rare. Jasper is found worldwide. Jasper with patterns reminiscent of landscapes is called picture jasper.

Fig. 4.9 Picture jasper from Idaho

ONYX: Chalcedony that is composed of relatively straight, parallel layers of different colors. When the dark layers (bands) are brown or brownish red, it's often called **SARDONYX.**

BLACK ONYX is not really onyx. It's just chalcedony that's been dyed black.

PETRIFIED WOOD: (Fossilized Wood, Agatized Wood): Wood that has been replaced by chalcedony.

SARD: Brown or brownish-red chalcedony. It's generally considered to be similar to carnelian but is darker and brown. There's no distinct dividing line between sard and carnelian. Brazil and Uruguay are sources of both varieties.

Care tips: Chalcedony is durable, and it's usually safe to clean it in ultrasonic cleaners. Soapy water is always safe. Chalcedony is affected by some acids, and heat may change the color.

Figs. 4.10 & 4.11 Left: an enlarged view of a Colombian emerald in dayligh Right: the same emerald viewed under long-wave ultraviolet light. The bl fluorescence helps identify the type (Gematrat) and extent of the filler. Sor fillers exhibit a yellow/orange fluorescence and others may show none. The tw digital images are from the AGL lab report in Chapter 15.

Emerald, Aquamarine & Other Beryls

In its pure form, beryl is colorless. But thanks to the presence of impurities, this mineral can be blue, green, pink, red, yellow or orange. Of all the beryls, emerald is the most highly valued and has the longest history. Aquamarine and yellow beryl have also had a long history, but it's hard to determine when they were first used. The orange, pink and red beryls have only been recognized as gems since the early 1900's.

EMERALD: By definition, emeralds are green. If they have a saturated green color and are transparent and eye-clean, they can be worth several thousand dollars per carat wholesale. Low-grade emerald can sell for as little as $10 per carat. It's normal for an emerald to be flawed with inclusions and cracks, especially if it has a deep green color. Nevertheless, clarity and transparency play a major role in emerald pricing.

Emeralds are routinely treated with oil, wax or epoxy-like substances to hide cracks and improve transparency. This is considered an acceptable trade practice as long as it's disclosed. Some fillers, however, are more preferred than others. In expensive emeralds, for example, oil is preferred over hardened epoxy fillers. It's impossible for most salespeople to know what an emerald has been filled with. They should, however, be able to tell you how to care for it. Reputable jewelers will stand behind their emeralds, and many will retreat the stones if necessary. For a much fuller discussion of emerald treatments, quality evaluation and identification, consult the *Ruby, Sapphire & Emerald Buying Guide* by Renée Newman.

Colombia is the most important source of top-grade emerald. High-quality emerald is also found in Zambia, Zimbabwe, Brazil and Pakistan, but not in the same quantities.

GREEN BERYL: Beryl that is light green. There is no agreed-upon criterion in the trade for distinguishing between green beryl and emerald. Likewise, there's no clear dividing line between green beryl and aquamarine.

AQUAMARINE: Most natural-color aquamarine is light bluish-green. Prior to the 1900's, this was the preferred color for the stone. Today aquamarine is routinely heat-treated to remove the green, thereby producing a permanently-colored blue stone. The more intense the blue color, the more valuable the stone. Aquamarines usually have a high transparency and clarity. In addition, they're durable and their color is evenly distributed.

Brazil is the main producer of aquamarine. Madagascar, Mozambique, Ukraine, Nigeria, Pakistan and Zambia are other major sources.

HELIODOR (YELLOW BERYL): Found in Madagascar, Brazil, Russia, Namibia and the U.S., this beryl is not uncommon. It has also been called golden beryl.

MORGANITE (PINK, ORANGE or PURPLE BERYL): The first morganite to be described was a pale pink variety found in California. Some of the finest, most intensely-colored morganite is found in Madagascar. Brazil is another important source, but the colors are usually lighter even though the crystals are much larger. Some morganite is heat-treated to intensify the color.

Fig. 4.12 Yellow beryl crystal. *Pendant and photo from Extreme Gioelli.*

RED BERYL (BIXBITE): This valuable beryl was discovered in Utah in 1906. Red beryl is sometimes erroneously called red emerald. Due to its rarity, it remains a collector gem.

Beware: Lab-grown emerald is sometimes sold as natural emerald. Light green beryl may be darkened by green oil, coated with green plastic or cemented together with green glue to look like a deep green emerald. Glass is often used to imitate emerald and aquamarine. Blue topaz is sometimes sold as aquamarine.

When buying an expensive emerald, find out if the filling enhancement has had a major impact on its clarity. You wouldn't want to pay, say, $6,000 for an emerald that in its unenhanced state is worth $600.

Care tips: Beryl is a relatively durable mineral and can be cleaned ultrasonically if it doesn't contain inclusions and cracks. Emeralds, however, typically have fractures, which can be enlarged with the vibration of ultrasonics and with hard knocks. In addition, ultrasonics can remove emerald fillers, making the stones look worse after cleaning. Clean emeralds with a damp cloth or spray with window cleaner and wipe dry. Do not soak emeralds in cleaning solutions because they can dissolve fillers.

Avoid high heat. It can make liquid inclusions expand, causing fracturing; it can dry out oil in emeralds; and it can produce fading in morganite.

Stones with fractures like those found in emeralds are not a good choice for everyday rings. Wear emeralds, instead, in necklaces, earrings and brooches, which won't be subjected to knocks and hard wear.

Garnet

Traditionally, people have considered garnets to be red, but they can also be various shades of green, yellow, orange, brown, pink or purple. The principal members of the garnet group are:

ANDRADITE: The best known andradite variety is **demantoid**, which was discovered in 1868 in Russia. It resembles an emerald with added brilliance and fire.

Good demantoid is not easy to find today. Some demantoid is mined in Mexico, Italy, Czechoslovakia and Arizona but the color tends to be yellowish, so it's not as highly prized as that found in Russia. The retail price of demantoid can range from about $400 to over $5000 per carat.

4.13 Hessonite garnet accented by Mali garnets. *Ring from Cynthia Rée Co.; photo by John Parrish.*

Fig. 4.14 Pyrope garnet. *Ring and photo from Linda Quinn.*

SPESSARTINE or "spessartite" which is sometimes used to refer to faceted spessartine: Spessartine is sometimes confused with yellow topaz or hessonite garnet. It can be yellowish orange to reddish orange, but the most valued color is orange with red overtones. One recent variety is called **mandarin garnet** and is mined in Namibia. Another new variety from Kashmir is appropriately called **kashmirine**.

Other sources include Sri Lanka, Brazil, Afghanistan, Myanmar, Madagascar, East Africa and California. Retail prices of top-grade material can be as high as $1000 per carat. Most spessartines, however, tend to sell for about $5 to $200 per carat.

ALMANDINE also called almandite: Almandines typically have a purplish color. Sources include Sri Lanka, India, Brazil, Australia, Tanzania, Madagascar and the United States. Star almandine is found in Idaho.

RHODOLITE: Rhodolite, a purplish red garnet is mined in Africa, Brazil, India and Sri Lanka. Tanzania is the major commercial source. Rhodolites can range in price from $5 to $250 per carat retail. Top-quality stones are clean, very transparent and saturated in color but not dark.

PYROPE (PIE rope): Pyrope is found throughout the world, with some of the best quality coming from the diamond mines of South Africa. As a result, it has sometimes been referred to as "cape ruby." "Arizona ruby" is a misnomer for pyrope from Arizona. Pyrope is a very affordable stone with retail prices ranging from about $5 to $100 per carat. The redder the stone, the more valuable it is. Eye-clean material is readily available.

MALI GARNET or **GRANDITE**: Marketed only since 1995, Mali garnets are found in western Africa in the Republic of Mali. They can be various shades of green, yellow or brown.

MALAIA (MALAYA): This distinctive orange variety may be reddish, pinkish or yellowish. It was found in East Africa in the search for rhodolite. Pinkish orange and orange with overtones of red are the most valued colors. Top qualities can retail for up to $500 whereas low-grade malaia sells for as little as $10 per carat.

COLOR-CHANGE GARNET is found in many different colors and displays a variation of color behavior. For example, it may be blue or green in daylight and red in incandescent light.

GROSSULAR: The most valued grossular variety is **tsavorite**, a transparent green garnet. It was discovered in Tanzania in 1968. Tsavorite is found in almost all shades of green but tends to be yellowish-green. When its color resembles that of fine emerald, it can wholesale for over $1500 per carat in sizes over 3 carats. Retail prices of smaller commercial quality stones can drop down to $100 per carat.

    Hessonite is a much less expensive variety of grossular that is sometimes called **cinnamon stone**. The colors are often brownish and can be red, orange, yellow or colorless. There are hessonite deposits in Sri Lanka, the U.S., Canada, Madagascar, Siberia and Brazil. Translucent and opaque grossular is used for beads, cabochons and carvings. The green material is sometimes called **Transvaal jade**, after its main source in South Africa. It has also been found in the USSR, Hungary and Italy.

Care tips: It's safe to clean garnets in ultrasonics if they don't have fractures or liquid inclusions. It's safer to just clean them with warm soapy water. Never boil or steam clean garnets. Abrupt temperature changes cause fracturing. They are slightly attacked by hydrofluoric acid, but otherwise they're resistant to chemicals. Garnets do not fade.

    A major advantage of garnets is that they're normally not treated with oil, plastic, wax, epoxy, dyes, glass-like fillings and other substances. When you buy a garnet, you're usually getting a truly natural gemstone.

Iolite

Before the 1980's, iolite was mainly considered a collector's stone because so little of it was being sold. Today, it's more readily available, and it's often used as a sapphire or tanzanite substitute because of its blue-violet color and lower price. You can find high-quality iolite for less than $200 per carat retail. Overly dark and flawed stones sell for much less.

Fig. 4.15 Iolite

Some people have referred to iolite as **water sapphire** because it resembles sapphire face-up and it looks clear or watery from the side. This effect is due to the way iolite polarizes light. In one direction the crystal typically appears dark blue or violet; in another it's colorless, gray or yellowish; and in a third direction it's light blue or violet.

Major sources: Most iolite comes from India, Sri Lanka, Tanzania and Brazil. Additional sources include Myanmar, Madagascar, Zimbabwe and Namibia.

Care tips: Clean with warm soapy water. Avoid ultrasonics and sudden changes of temperature. Iolite is attacked by acids and it's susceptible to cleaving (cracking) if it's hit against something.

Jade (Jadeite & Nephrite)

Jade refers to two different minerals—**jadeite** and **nephrite.** Both stones are rocks (aggregates)—masses of tightly interlocking crystals. However, they have different chemical compositions and properties. Jadeite is a little harder and denser, and as a result can take a higher polish than nephrite. Neither stone is very hard, compared to diamond and ruby. However, both jades are unusually tough—resistant to breakage and chipping. Nephrite, however, is slightly stronger.

Jadeite is more valuable and rare than nephrite. When it's very translucent and has a strong emerald-green color, it's often called imperial jade. Jadeite is found in a variety of colors—lavender, white, gray, yellow, orange, brownish-red, black and many shades of green. Today, jadeite is usually the jade chosen for fine jewelry. Its intrinsic value is generally the basis for its price. Nephrite, on the other hand, is mainly valued for its antiquity and carving excellence.

Nephrite is plentiful and most of it is grayish green—typically forest green or olive green. It can also be white, gray, black, brown, yellow or beige. Most nephrite is very affordable. For example, you can easily find nephrite costume jewelry ranging from $10 to $50. The antique value of old nephrite pieces often outweighs their intrinsic worth.

Evaluation of Jade

COLOR: An intense green with a medium to medium-dark tone is the most valued. As the color becomes lighter, darker, more grayish or brownish or yellowish, the value decreases. Lavender is the next most valued hue, followed by red, yellow, white and black. Prior to the importation of Burmese jadeite into China, white nephrite was the most coveted jade.

Fig. 4.16 Top-quality green jade f[r] Mason-Kay. *Photo by Richard Rub[y]*

Green nephrite is typically grayish, blackish or brownish. The more it approaches a pure green, the more desirable it is.

COLOR UNIFORMITY: In top quality jade, the color is uniform throughout the stone. The more uneven or blotchy the color is, the lower the value. Multi-colored jade, however, can be very expensive if the colors are intense and distinct. The most desired color combinations are green and lavender, orange and green, or white with strong green (**moss-in-snow** jade).

TRANSPARENCY: The best jade is either near transparent or highly translucent. As the transparency of jade decreases, so does its value, with opaque jade being worth the least.

CLARITY: Fine jade is free of flaws such as cracks, included foreign material, and spots which reduce beauty or durability. The

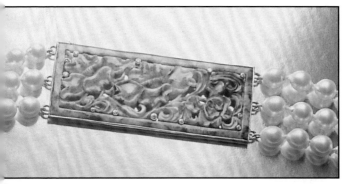

Fig. 4.17 Jadeite neckpiece. *Necklace from Richard Kimball; photo by Steve Ramsey.*

number, size, color, position and nature of flaws determines the clarity of a stone. Cracks that break the surface or that are visible internally are particularly detrimental to the value.

TEXTURE: Since jade is composed of interwoven crystals, it can have a texture that ranges from fine to coarse. The finer and more tightly interwoven the crystal components are, the better the jade.

SHAPE: The best jade is cut into cabochons. Ovals and rounds normally sell for more than rectangular, marquise and pear shapes. Smooth uncarved pieces are more valuable than carved ones. Carving allows the removal of flaws from inferior material.

CUT QUALITY: Moderately curved cabochons tend to be more valued than flat or very high ones. Symmetrical cabochons with balanced proportions are the most desired. Intricate, high-quality carving is naturally more valued than shoddy, quick carving.

SIZE: Since large, fine quality jadeite is rare, size plays a role in increasing its value. The thickness of good jadeite is also important. If a jadeite cabochon is thinner than 2 mm or smaller than 8 x 6 mm, there can be a considerable deduction in its per-carat value.

POLISH & FINISH: The more brilliant the polish and the smoother the surface, the better the stone is.

Jade Treatments

Waxing: This is commonly done after the final polish to improve luster and hide pits and cracks. Heat and strong solvents will undo this treatment. Material with only a superficial waxing is often called **A jade** and is well-accepted by the trade.

Dyeing: This is done to add green or lavender color to white or light-colored jade. Blueberry juice is a common dye for lavender jade. It looks good at first but it can fade in sunlight. Dyed jade is called **C Jade** and is not accepted as fine jade.

Heating: Dark green nephrite may be treated by this method to lighten the color of dark-green material. Red jade can be heated to increase redness, but the usual result is a dull brown, and transparency is reduced in the process.

Bleaching and polymer impregnation: This relatively new treatment removes brown from jade, making white colors whiter and green colors brighter. The jade is first soaked and bleached in chemicals. Then the bleached jade is impregnated with a wax or synthetic resin to fill voids created from the bleaching process. The resulting material is called **B jade**. Sometimes dye is used before impregnation and other times it's added to the filler. Don't plan on handing bleached jade down to future generations; it has durability problems and will discolor with time.

Major sources: Myanmar has been the main source of jadeite since the late 18th century. Some jadeite is also mined in Russia, Japan and California; but the finest quality comes from Myanmar.

    The oldest known source of nephrite is Xinjiang Province in China. Nephrite is also found in New Zealand, Taiwan, British Columbia, Australia, Poland, Germany, India, Zimbabwe, Mexico, Alaska, California and Wyoming.

Beware: Sellers are supposed to disclose treatments but not all do. Therefore ask for treatment information, particularly when buying high-priced jadeite. If a store claims their jade is only waxed and otherwise untreated, have them write this on the receipt. If you're buying quality jade jewelry, check if it has open back settings to let light through the stone. Closed backs are typically a sign that the jade is of low value or that something is being hidden. For example, it might be hiding the back of a jadeite triplet—an assembled stone consisting of a thin hollow cabochon of translucent grayish-white jadeite that's coated inside with a thin, green jelly-like substance and cemented to a piece of flat oval jade. When mounted it looks like an imperial jadeite cabochon. You're much more likely to encounter dyed jade, than jadeite triplets.

Some common jade imitations are serpentine, chrysoprase, grossular garnet and dyed chalcedony.

Care tips: Jade can be safely cleaned in soapy water, ultrasonics and steamers. It reacts slightly to warm acids. Since jade has a lower hardness than gems such as sapphire, emerald and topaz, it can get scratched more easily. Jewelers can eliminate the scratches and restore the luster by polishing the jade.

Jade, however, is very durable. In fact, there is no other gem that's as resistant to breakage and chipping as jade.

Kunzite (Spodumene)

Kunzite is pink to purple in color and is typically eye-clean and low priced. You can find well-cut, light pink stones of high clarity for under $60 per carat retail. Stones with a more saturated color are available, but they can be difficult to find in North America or Europe. These stones are often reserved for buyers in Japan. Some kunzite is irradiated to intensify its color. Unfortunately, the color fades over time when exposed to strong light or heat.

Fig. 4.18 Kunzite

Major sources: Kunzite and other spodumene varieties are mined in Afghanistan, Pakistan, Brazil, Madagascar and the U.S.

Care tips: Clean with soapy water. Avoid ultrasonics and sudden temperature changes. Kunzite can crack easily if it's knocked against a surface. It may fade in light, and it's sensitive to heat and hydrofluoric acid.

Lapis Lazuli

Fig. 4.19 Lapis globe. *Photo by Lange.*

Lapis lazuli is a rock made up of several different minerals. The most valued lapis has a natural, even, deep violet-blue color that is free of white calcite veining. It also has a high polish and a bit of pyrite. Dyed lapis is the least valuable type. Dye is used to improve the color and to hide white calcite. Often, the dye is not very stable and may rub off on your skin. A wax coating is commonly used to seal in the dye and to make the polish look better. It's not always possible for salespeople to know if lapis has been dyed. However, if they claim the color is natural and the stone is untreated, have them write this on the receipt. Generally, most lapis beads are dyed. Dye can frequently be detected by rubbing the stone with cotton dipped in fingernail polish remover or alcohol. Never do this in a conspicuous spot and always get permission first.

Major sources: For over 5000 years, lapis lazuli (lapis) has been mined in Northeastern Afghanistan. This is still the world's most important source both in terms of quality and quantity.

The second most important source of lapis is Chile. However, Chilean lapis tends to contain a lot of white calcite and the color can be relatively light. Consequently it's often dyed.

Beware: German and Swiss lapis are not lapis lazuli. They're blue dyed jasper, the most widely used lapis imitation. Glass, plastic and sodalite are also used to imitate lapis. The Gilson company produces another imitation lapis.

Care tips: Clean with warm soapy water but don't soak. Ultrasonics and steamers are risky cleaning methods. Avoid rough wear, heat and acids.

Malachite

Malachite is usually banded with differing shades of green in agate-like patterns. It's attractive, yet low-priced. You should be able to find, for example, a nice-quality 12 x 10 mm cabochon for less than $15. Often, malachite is banded and intermixed with other copper minerals such as blue azurite. The resulting material is called **azurmalachite**.

Major Sources: DR Congo is the major producer of malachite. Other sources include Russia, Zambia, Namibia, Arizona, New Mexico and Australia.

Beware: Synthetic malachite is produced in Russia. Malachite is so inexpensive that it's not often imitated.

Sometimes, malachite is impregnated with wax or epoxy to improve the polish and hide small cracks.

Care tips: Malachite can easily break or scratch. It's also sensitive to heat, acids and ammonia. Never clean it ultrasonically; wipe it with lukewarm, soapy water and rinse.

Fig. 4.20 Malachite

Moonstone & Some Other Feldspars

MOONSTONE: This gem is noted for a floating light effect and sheen called **adularescence**, which has been compared to the light of the moon. High moonstone cabochons may resemble cat's-eye gems due to the concentration of light along the top of the stone.

Moonstone is typically white, colorless or light grayish blue, but it may also be yellow, orange, brown, blue or green. It ranges from near transparent to almost opaque. The most valued stones are blue and near transparent—sometimes $100 a carat. Translucent white stones can cost less than $5 per carat.

LABRADORITE: This name most often refers to a dark, opaque feldspar, first found in Labrador, that displays a flash of color(s) when viewed at certain angles. This optical effect, which is called

Fig. 4.21 Moonstone   **Fig. 4.22** Oregon sunstone

labradorescence, is typically bright blue, but it can also be green, yellow, orange or rarely purple.

SUNSTONE: There are two main types of sunstone. The best known, aventurine feldspar, is opaque and has glittery red or golden inclusions. Another transparent type is orange, yellow, red or colorless. It is the state gem of Oregon.

AMAZONITE (Amazon Stone): A bluish-green variety, this is sometimes sold as "Pikes Peak jade" in Colorado. It's also found in Virginia, India, Russia and Africa.

Major sources: Most moonstone comes from India, Myanmar and Sri Lanka. Aventurine feldspar (sunstone) is found in India, Canada, Norway, Siberia and the USA. Transparent sunstone is mined in Oregon. Labradorite is named after its most famous source, Labrador, Newfoundland.

Care tips: Clean with soapy water. Never clean feldspar with an ultrasonic cleaner, steamer or chemicals. The *GIA Gem Reference Guide* rates feldspar's toughness as poor, so don't wear it in everyday rings. Heat and knocks cause it to crack. In fact, "feldspar" is derived from "field" and "spar," a word that refers to any shiny rock that splits easily.

Opal

When comparing opal prices, find out what type of opal you're looking at. Here are the various types:

COMMON OPAL and **POTCH:** Opal with **no** play-of-color (shifting of spectral colors) and a translucent to opaque transparency. Opal with a play-of-color, the most popular kind, is called **precious opal** by many opal dealers.

LIGHT OPAL: Opal with a play-of-color and a light body color. **White opal** is the most common type. It typically has an off-white background color and can be translucent to opaque. Milky white stones with little play-of-color are used in budget-priced jewelry. White opals with a brilliant play-of-color can retail for a few hundred dollars per carat. When an opal has a high transparency, a near colorless body color and a distinct play-of-color, then it's called a **crystal opal**. This is the most valued light opal. In its highest qualities it can cost more than $2500 per carat retail.

BOULDER OPAL: Opal that is still attached to the rock (usually ironstone) in which it is found. Boulder opal, which can resemble either light or dark opal, is typically cut in irregular shapes. Gem quality boulder opal may sell for $5,000 to $50,000 per piece, but you can get attractive stones for a few hundred dollars. Boulder opal is mined in Queensland, Australia.

BLACK (DARK) OPAL: A generic term for any opal with a play-of-color against a dark background. If the stone is transparent to semi-transparent and dark with a play-of-color, the stone is a **black crystal opal**. Today top-grade black opal can sell for as much as $15,000 a carat. It's found in Lightning Ridge, Australia.

MATRIX OPAL or **OPAL-IN-MATRIX:** Stones with lines or spots of opal randomly scattered through the **matrix** (the rock in which a mineral, fossil or pebble is found). The most common type is a porous opal from Andamooka, Australia, which is often dyed black to simulate black opal. Yowah opal, another type of matrix opal, is completely natural and is mined in Yowah, South Queensland. Matrix opal normally sells for much less than boulder opal.

Fig. 4.23 Australian boulder opals. *Photo and opals from Robert Shapiro.*

Fig. 4.24 Yowah opals. *P and pendant from Neshama*

FIRE OPAL: A transparent to translucent opal with a red, orange, yellow or brownish body color both with or without a play-of-color. Mexico is the principal source. The most valued fire opal is reddish orange, transparent, and has a play-of-color within the stone. This quality can retail for as much as $300 per carat. Low quality brownish stones may sell for $5 per carat.

Treatments, Assembled Stones, Etc.

Beware: Opal is sometimes impregnated with oil, wax or plastic to improve the play-of-color and to prevent or disguise cracking. The plastic is stable, but the oil and wax isn't. There are various techniques for creating the appearance of black opal. These include smoke impregnation, backing with black or colored paint, and treatment with dye, silver nitrate or sugar carbonized by acid. These treatments are not well accepted by the trade because they're usually done to deceive buyers. When buying opal, asked if it's been treated or enhanced in any way. If it's untreated opal, ask the seller to write this on the receipt.

Occasionally sellers try to pass off doublets as boulder opal. An **opal doublet** is a thin slice of opal cemented usually with black glue to another material such as potch opal, ironstone, chalcedony or glass. If this doublet also has a protective top of colorless quartz or glass, it's called an **opal triplet** or a **triplet opal**. Doublets are normally more expensive than triplets because more opal is used but less expensive than boulder opals, which have a naturally attached backing. Often you can detect the man-made stones by looking at them from the side. A doublet typically has a straight separation line whereas a boulder opal has a crooked one.

There are also fake opal stones. One is called **Slocum Stone** and another **Opalite**. Hong Kong is a major producer of imitation opal. Synthetic opal is grown in Japan and Russia.

Factors Which Affect Opal Value

OPAL TYPE: Solid black opal is more expensive than boulder opal if similar qualities and colors of each category are compared. Matrix opals and assembled stones are the least expensive types. There's a great difference in price between a natural and an assembled opal of similar appearance, so it's important to have salespeople identify the type of opal verbally and on the receipt.

BODY TONE: (The darkness or lightness of the background color): Black opal is more expensive than light opal of like quality. With black and boulder opal, generally the darker the background the more valuable the stone is. When determining body tone, look at the top of the stone.

BRILLIANCE: The overall brightness and intensity of the play-of-color. The more brilliant the flashes of color, the better the stone. Examine brilliance both under a consistent light source and away from it. Stones that maintain their brightness away from light are the most highly valued. Brilliance is one of the most important value factors.

PLAY OF COLOR: The dominant color(s) and the combination of colors are both important. Intense red is the most rare and therefore the most prized color. In terms of value, it's followed by orange, green and blue, the most plentiful color. The way in which different color combinations are priced can vary from one dealer to another. Any type of play-of-color can be desirable, as long as the colors are intense and not dull when viewed face up.

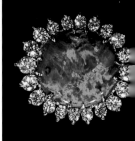

Fig. 4.25 A crystal opal with a blue play of color. On a white background, it looks white and blue because of its transparency. *Designed by Avara Yaron; photo & brooch from Neshama.*

Fig. 4.26 A black opal with tense color. *Opal from Royal Antique Jewelry, pho. Harold & Erica Van Pelt.*

COLOR PATTERN: The diffracted colors in opals are displayed in various patterns such as **pinfire**—small pin-point like color specks and **flashfire**—larger splashes of color, usually irregular in shape; Pinfire and small type patterns are generally less desirable than broad patterns or large flashes.

TRANSPARENCY: For light opal and fire opal, the higher the transparency, the more valuable the stone. For black opal, the opaque, blacker stones tend to be more highly valued than those with greater transparency.

SHAPE: The most sought-after traditional shape is a well-formed oval. It tends to bring a higher price than other shapes because it's in greater demand, it's easier to set, and valuable opal material is sacrificed when stones are cut as ovals. Many designers, however, prefer other shapes, especially freeforms. Unusual freeforms may sell for more than ovals, especially after they're mounted.

CUT: All else being equal, domed cabochons tend to be more valued than flat ones. Excessive weight on the bottom and a thin or unsymmetrical profile can all reduce the value of an opal.

IMPERFECTIONS: Opal value decreases when there are eye-visible imperfections on the top of the stone. The larger and more noticeable they are, the greater their impact on value. Cracks drastically reduce value. A common opal flaw is **crazing**—a thin, network of fractures that resembles a spider web. When deep, it has a serious impact on price.

SIZE & CARAT WEIGHT: Stones under a carat are generally worth less per carat than larger ones. If a stone is unusually large, it may be worth less per carat than stones more suitable for general jewelry use. Boulder opals are typically priced by size rather than carat weight. The larger the opal the higher the price.

Major sources: Most of the world's opal comes from Australia. Opal is also found in Mexico, Brazil, the U.S., Japan and Honduras, but the finest quality is produced in Australia.

Care tips: Since opals are relatively soft and fragile, they require special care. Avoid heat and sudden changes of temperature. Do not wear them while sunbathing or set them on a sunny window sill or under hot lights. Don't clean them in ultrasonics. Instead, wash them in water with a mild soap and soft cloth. (Opal doublets and triplets, however, should not be immersed in water.)

Peridot

Peridot is attractive, yet affordable. You can purchase a high quality peridot for less than $150 per carat retail. The greener the stone and the better the clarity, the higher the value.

Major sources: The oldest source of peridot is St. John's Island, Egypt, in the Red Sea. Pakistan and Arizona are the main sources today. Other important deposits are in China and Myanmar.

Beware: Glass and synthetic spinel are occasionally used to imitate peridot. Peridot is normally not treated, but on rare occasions it has been fracture filled to improve clarity.

Fig. 4.27 Peridot. *Pendant from Cynthia Renée Co.; photo by John Parrish.*

Care tips: Clean with soapy water. Ultrasonics are risky. Sudden temperature changes or uneven heat can cause fracturing. Jeweler's pickling solutions and some acids will attack peridot.

Ruby & Sapphire (Corundum)

Ruby and sapphire are the same mineral—corundum, so they have the same physical characteristics. Color is what distinguishes ruby from sapphire. Rubies are red and sapphires are either blue or another color such as green, orange, pink, yellow, purple, colorless or black (sapphire colors other than blue are called **fancy colors** and are identified by color, e.g., green sapphire).

RUBY: Dealers disagree on whether orangy-red rubies are better than those· which are red or purplish-red. However, they agree that a strong red fluorescence is desirable and that top-grade stones should have a minimal amount of black, gray or brown masking the red. Medium to medium-dark tones are generally preferred by the trade. The highest percentage of stones that have met these color criteria are from the Mogok area of Myanmar (Burma).

Fig. 4.28 Ruby with excellent cc *Photo from Asian Institute of C ological Sciences (AIGS).*

But don't assume, that a ruby is good quality if it originates from Mogok. Likewise, don't assume that rubies from other localities such as Thailand, Cambodia, Sri Lanka, Vietnam, Tanzania and Kenya must be inferior. High-quality material has originated from all of these countries.

Large rubies have sold for as much as $200,000 per carat, but good rubies with inclusions in the 1-carat range are available for $3000–$4000 per carat. You can also find nearly opaque rubies for as low as $10 per carat. A premium may be charged if a high-grade stone originates from Mogok or shows no evidence of heat treatment, providing it has a lab report from a respected lab. Rubies are commonly heat-treated to improve color and/or clarity. Diffusion treatment, glass fillings, oils or dyes usually have a negative impact on value (see Chapter 2).

SAPPHIRE: When used by itself, the term **sapphire** normally refers to the blue variety. In its highest qualities, it's more expensive than the other varieties. Top-quality Kashmir sapphires, for example, can wholesale for over $25,000 a carat (mining in Kashmir has been extremely limited for decades).

Opinions differ as to what is the best sapphire hue. Some say blue, others say violetish blue. Most dealers agree, however, that greenish blues are less valuable. Dealers also have different tone preferences. Some prefer medium tones of blue while others prefer medium-dark tones. Pale, blackish or grayish stones, however, cost the least. Good sapphires in the one-carat range are available for $1000–$2000 retail.

Fig. 4.29 Unheated Burmese sapphire with excellent color. *Sapphire and photo from Fred Mouawad.*

Major producers of blue sapphire are Myanmar, Sri Lanka, Thailand, Cambodia, Madagascar and Australia. Sapphire is also mined in China, Colombia, Kenya, Malawi, Montana, Nigeria, Tanzania and Vietnam. The lowest priced stones often come from Australia because they tend to be overly dark and have low transparency.

Sapphires are usually heat treated. Their outer surface is sometimes darkened by diffusion treatment, but this must always be disclosed. Sapphires with surface-reaching fractures are occasionally oiled to improve clarity. This should also be disclosed.

PADPARADSCHA: a light to medium-toned, orange-pink sapphire found in Sri Lanka. It's the rarest and most prized of all the fancy sapphires. Don't expect to find it in a jewelry store. In their finest qualities, true padparadschas in large sizes can wholesale for over $20,000 per carat.

PINK SAPPHIRE: Next to the padparadscha, this is the most highly prized of all the fancy sapphires. Since "pink" is a synonym of "light red" and since fine rubies cost more than sapphires, many Asian dealers prefer to call pink sapphires rubies. The jewelry trade in western countries prefers to treat the pink sapphire as a unique stone with its own merits, rather than as a

Fig. 4.30 Sapphires from Tanzania and Sri Lanka

lower-priced ruby. High-quality pink sapphires can cost several thousand dollars per carat. The most valuable pink sapphires have a saturated hot pink color. As the stones get lighter, more brownish or more purple, their value decreases.

Sri Lanka, Burma and Madagascar are the most important sources of pink sapphire, but it is also mined in countries such as Tanzania and Vietnam.

ORANGE, GREEN, PURPLE, or YELLOW SAPPHIRE: Tanzania, Sri Lanka, Thailand and Montana are important sources of these sapphires. A high percentage of green sapphire is found in Australia. Of these four sapphire colors, orange is the most valued; green is typically the lowest priced; and yellow is usually the most readily available.

Fig. 4.31 Yellow sapphires. *Earrings from Cynthia Renée Co.; photo by John Parrish.*

WHITE SAPPHIRE (colorless sapphire): This sapphire is produced by heat treating light-colored sapphire. Natural sapphire normally has a trace of color. In recent years, white sapphire has become popular as a diamond substitute. Unlike cubic zirconia, white sapphire is mined from the earth rather than made in a lab.

STAR SAPPHIRE AND STAR RUBY: Star corundum with a fine blue or red color is rare. Gray, maroon and black-star stones are easier to find, and their prices can be relatively low.

Beware: There's a lot of synthetic ruby and sapphire on the market which is sometimes identified as natural. If a ruby is large and flawless, assume it's lab-grown. Normally, large rubies and most large sapphires have inclusions. Lab-grown ruby may also have inclusions.

Not all sellers disclose gem treatments and some do not know what treatments their stones have undergone. The heat treatment of rubies and sapphires is an accepted trade practice and often cannot be identified. Diffusion treatment, oiling and cavity filling can be identified by gem labs but these treatments are not well accepted. It's more difficult to detect glassy residues in fractures which result from heat treatment. Promotional quality rubies typically have glassy residues in their fractures. Dealers don't want the residue to be present in their high quality stones.

Care tips: Rubies and sapphires can be safely cleaned in ultrasonics and steamers provided they're not oiled, cavity filled or badly flawed. One exception is black-star sapphire, which tends to be fragile. Cleaning corundum with soap and water is safe. Heat treated ruby and sapphire is stable to light, but some irradiated orange and yellow sapphires may fade. Corundum is resistant to most chemicals. However, soldering flux or pickling solutions containing borax will etch the surface of the stone.

Rubies and sapphires are hard, strong and generally very durable. In fact, the only natural gemstone that surpasses them in hardness is diamond.

More detailed information on corundum is available in the *Ruby, Sapphire & Emerald Buying Guide* by Renée Newman and in *Ruby & Sapphire* by Richard W. Hughes.

Spinel

Custom jewelers and collectors who like unusual gems appreciate spinel. It's available in a variety of colors.

RED SPINEL: Red is the most valued spinel color. The best red spinels resemble a high-quality ruby and usually come from Myanmar. High-quality red spinels can retail for over $2500 per carat. Low-quality brownish stones are available for under $100 a carat. Prices for stones above 10 carats are negotiable.

PINK SPINEL: This often sells for about one-third to one-half the price of red spinel. The lighter the color the lower the price.

ORANGE SPINEL: Its color ranges from yellow-orange to red-orange. This spinel is sometimes called **flame spinel**.

BLUE SPINEL: Fine blue colors are rare and can retail for over $2000 per carat. This spinel tends to be grayish or dark. In an attempt to lighten the color, stones are often cut shallow.

COLOR-SHIFT SPINEL: A rare stone, it's grayish-blue in daylight and purplish-blue under incandescent light-bulbs.

Geographic sources: Myanmar and Sri Lanka are the main sources of spinel. Other localities are Afghanistan, Thailand, Cambodia, Tanzania, Russia and Vietnam. Spinel is often a by-product of the search for ruby and sapphire.

Fig. 4.32 Spinels in a pendar Gary Dulac. *Photo by Azad.*

Beware: Synthetic spinel may be sold as natural spinel.

Care tips: Spinel can be cleaned in ultrasonics, steamers and warm soapy water. Its color is stable to light, but some light colored stones may fade under intense heat. It doesn't react to chemicals. Overall, spinel is durable, comparatively hard and typically has a better clarity and brilliance than a ruby.

Tanzanite

Tanzanite was discovered in the 1960's in the foothills of Africa's Mt. Kilimanjaro. Later, Henry Platt, vice-president and director of Tiffany's, named the stone after its country of origin, Tanzania. As with sapphire, the unmodified "tanzanite" refers to the blue or violet variety, whereas other colors must be specified.

4.33 A 33-carat emerald-cut tanzanite

Fig. 4.34 A faceted tanzanite flanked by two unheated and unpolished tanzanite crystals. The crystals change color from blue to purple as they're moved.

Some dealers feel that the most desirable tanzanite color is a deep blue with a faint purple secondary color. Others prefer an equal mix of blue and purple. Most dealers would agree, though, that blue stones are worth more than those which are purple. Light lavender stones are priced the lowest. You can find high-quality, deep-blue tanzanites with purple overtones for less than $1400 per carat retail. Tanzanite prices fluctuate a lot. Most tanzanite is heat-treated to intensify the color and/or eliminate brown, gray or green.

Beware: There are some good tanzanite imitations, which may be glass, synthetic forsterite, Coranite™ (synthetic corundum), or Tanavyte™ (synthetic garnet). Sometimes these imitations are sold as synthetic tanzanite. So far, no one has been able to synthesize tanzanite in a laboratory.

Geographic sources: Although some tanzanite is found in Kenya, Tanzania is considered the sole commercial source of tanzanite.

Care tips: Clean tanzanite in warm, soapy water. Avoid ultrasonics and steamers. Tanzanite is stable to light but reacts to hydrochloric and hydrofluoric acid. The biggest problem with tanzanite is that it's very susceptible to cracking when bumped or knocked. That combined with its tendency to abrade makes it inappropriate for wear in everyday rings. It's an impressive stone, however, for necklaces, earrings and brooches.

Topaz

Most topaz is light brown when mined and then turns colorless after exposure to light or low heat. Otherwise it tends to be pale blue. Consequently, yellow, orange and pink topaz are highly regarded. Crystals weighing several kilos are common.

PINK to RED TOPAZ: Top-grade red or strong pink topaz is the most valuable type of topaz. The redder and more saturated the color, the rarer and more costly the stone. Natural-color stones, which generally come from Pakistan, can sell for much more than those which are treated. Most pink topaz is heated brownish-yellow topaz from Brazil.

4.35 Blue topaz. *Pendant & photo Murphy Design; design—Lori Braun.*

Fig. 4.36 Imperial topaz (center) and pink topaz side stones. *Ring from Cynthia Renée Co.; photo by John Parrish.*

GOLDEN YELLOW to ORANGE TOPAZ: When this variety is intensely colored and has reddish or pink overtones, it is called **imperial topaz** and can retail from about $200 to over $2000 per carat. Stones that lack pink highlights or have a low color saturation are less valuable.

BLUE to GREEN TOPAZ: Produced by irradiating and then heating certain colorless material, blue topaz can look like fine aquamarine, but most is a stronger blue and looks less natural. Ever since the market was flooded with this topaz, its price has dropped to levels below $20 a carat.

Geographic sources: The world's largest producer of topaz is the state of Minas Gerais in Brazil. For almost 300 years, its Ouro Preto district has supplied the world with yellow, orange and pink topaz. Other sources include Pakistan, Afghanistan, Sri Lanka, Mexico, Australia, Myanmar, the Ukraine and the U.S.

Beware: Citrine quartz is often sold as "quartz topaz" or even "topaz" to make it sound more expensive. Therefore, when buying topaz, ask the seller to specify on the receipt that it is genuine topaz and not quartz or another gemstone.

Care tips: Clean with warm soapy water. Avoid ultrasonics, steamers, strong heat and sudden changes of temperature. Topaz is relatively hard, but cracks easily when dropped or knocked.

Tourmaline (a group of mineral species)

No other gemstone offers buyers a wider variety of colors than tourmaline. Besides being found in every color of the rainbow, tourmaline may also be multicolored in one piece. Some of the species and varieties of tourmaline are listed below:

GREEN TOURMALINE: This variety is plentiful and comes in a wide range of shades. It tends to appear very dark and non-transparent in one direction. To lighten and improve the color, green tourmaline is commonly heat-treated. Stones that are blackish and yellowish are the least expensive. Those with an intense green color resembling a good emerald cost the most.

Top-color green tourmalines are found in Tanzania and are called **chrome tourmalines**. Eye-clean green tourmaline is readily available. Therefore, good-quality stones are expected to have a high clarity. Top quality chrome tourmaline can retail for as much as $2000 per carat. Most green tourmaline, however, is quite affordable, with retail prices ranging from about $20 in very low qualities to $400 per carat in better stones

PINK or RED TOURMALINE: The discovery of pink tourmaline in southern California in 1898 helped popularize this stone. Red and pink tourmaline are also mined in Afghanistan, Brazil, Nigeria and Madagascar. **RUBELLITE** is a trade name applied to red tourmaline. True-red rubellites often have a low clarity. Clean rubellites with a strong red color can wholesale for over $1000 per carat.

Pink and red tourmalines from areas other than Nigeria are commonly irradiated to intensify their color. The stones are not radioactive and the color is relatively stable. However, strong heat like that from a display window or a jeweler's torch can cause the color to fade. Sometimes rubellite is treated with fillers to improve its clarity. Even when treated, you should expect it to have a lower clarity than other transparent tourmalines.

BLUE TOURMALINE (INDICOLITE or INDIGOLITE): Indicolite comes in various shades of blue, but frequently, it's a dark greenish or grayish blue. The color is often lightened with heat treatment. A brighter turquoise-blue material has been found in Northeastern Brazil in the state of Paraíba. It's called **Paraíba**

4.37 Tourmalines. *Rings created photographed by Linda Quinn.*

Fig. 4.38 Red tourmaline. *Ring designed by Tiziano Andorno; photo from Extreme Gioelli.*

tourmaline and is the rarest and most expensive tourmaline. In its finest qualities, it has wholesaled for over $5,000 per carat. Paraíba tourmaline can also have an intense green or violet color. Don't expect to find it in your local jewelry store. Indicolite costs less, ranging in price from about $100 to $800 retail per carat.

YELLOW, ORANGE, BROWN or GOLDEN TOURMALINE: Yellow and orange tourmaline occur naturally but are sometimes produced by irradiating light yellow or green tourmaline. Heat can cause the resulting color to fade. The orange and yellow stones may retail for about $30 to $350 per carat. Brown tourmaline tends to be less expensive.

BICOLORED or MULTICOLORED TOURMALINE: The pink and green variety is the most common type, but stones can also be pink and colorless or blue and green. Some stones have more than two colors. The most valued stones have distinct saturated colors with sharp boundaries and no fractures. Green and pink slices of crystal tourmaline that have concentric color banding are called **watermelon tourmaline**.

CAT'S-EYE TOURMALINE: This is found in a variety of colors but pink and green are less difficult to find than red or blue colors.

Cat's-eye tourmaline is occasionally treated with epoxy fillers to improve transparency and seal the tubes causing the cat's-eye. The fillers prevent dirt from entering the tubes.

Geographic Sources: Tourmaline has been found in significant quantities in Brazil, Afghanistan, Pakistan, Tanzania, Namibia, Madagascar, China, Sri Lanka, Nigeria, California and Russia.

Beware: Glass and synthetic spinel are sometimes sold as tourmaline by street vendors in countries such as Brazil.

Care tips: Clean tourmaline with warm soapy water. Ultrasonics are considered risky for this stone. Avoid strong heat because it may alter the color; sudden temperature changes may also cause fracturing. Tourmaline does not react to chemicals. It's normally stable to light, but some irradiated stones may fade with prolonged exposure.

Turquoise

The most highly valued turquoise is untreated and dense and has an even, intense sky-blue color. Usually this type of material is from Iran. The value is reduced if the color is green or pale or if inclusions or lines called "spider-webbing" are present. Some people, though, prefer greenish colors and patterned turquoise. Prices can range from $1 a stone to a few hundred dollars for a top-quality, untreated cabochon. In the 1970's, the same cab might have sold for $2000. Turquoise in genuine Indian jewelry or antique pieces may be worth a lot more than loose stones of the same quality.

Natural turquoise has stability problems. If it's not from Iran and it's not treated, it may turn green, white or occasionally brown within a year after it's mined. Porous material can crack or crumble. This is why almost all of the turquoise sold today has been treated—usually with a plastic substance designed to prevent discoloration and increase durability. A colorant may be added to improve the color. Sometimes turquoise is impregnated with wax to deepen the color and decrease porosity. However, the wax can pick up dirt and gradually discolor. When buying turquoise, assume it has been treated unless you're dealing with a knowled-

4.39 Turquoise earrings designed vara Yaron. *Photo from Neshama.*

Fig. 4.40 Arizona turquoise. *Ring and photo from The Roxx Limited.*

geable, trustworthy seller who writes on the receipt "untreated natural turquoise."

Major sources: The best turquoise occurs in northeast Iran near Nishapur, where it has been mined for over 3000 years. The material there is typically more stable and blue than that of other sources—China, Mexico, the Sinai Peninsula and Southwestern USA, the main producer.

Beware: Turquoise is imitated by plastic, glass, dyed chalcedony, dyed howlite, and a reconstructed turquoise made from turquoise power bonded with plastic. There's also a lab-grown turquoise, which is produced by Gilson. Sometimes liquid black shoe polish is used to create matrix patterns in turquoise.

Care tips: Clean with soapy water, but don't soak it. Avoid ultrasonics and steamers. Also avoid heat and chemicals. Perspiration, skin oils and cosmetics may turn blue turquoise green.

Zircon

Zircon is not the same as cubic zirconia (CZ). Zircon is a natural gemstone with exceptional brilliance and a diamond-like luster. Cubic zirconia is a synthetic stone with a different chemical composition. Zircon is found in a variety of colors.

Fig. 4.41 Zircons

BLUE ZIRCON: It often resembles aquamarine and blue topaz but has more fire and brilliance. The blue color results from heating brownish zircon. Blue zircon sold in jewelry stores is heat treated and susceptible to abrasions, especially when mounted in rings. Retail prices can range from $20 to $500 per carat depending on size and quality.

GREEN ZIRCON: Found mostly in Sri Lanka, this zircon is often grayish or yellowish. It's not uncommon for street vendors to sell it as green tourmaline or green sapphire. A curious property of green zircon is that it usually emits some level of natural radioactivity.

YELLOW, ORANGE, BROWN-RED & VIOLET ZIRCON: In their natural state, these zircons tend to be either brownish or pale. Heat treatment can intensify the color and reduce brown tints. To verify color stability, dealers sometimes expose them for several days to the sun.

Geographic sources: Three of the main sources of zircon are Cambodia, Thailand and Sri Lanka. It's also found in Vietnam, Myanmar, Tanzania, France and Australia. Bangkok is the world's cutting and marketing center for zircon.

Care tips: Clean with warm soapy water. Ultrasonics are risky cleaning methods. According to the GIA *Gem Reference Guide,* page 262, the toughness of untreated stones is fair to good whereas that of heat-treated stones is poor to fair. This means zircons can easily abrade and chip. Some heat-treated stones may revert to their original color. Zircon is resistant to chemicals.

5

Diamonds

Diamond Price Factors in a Nutshell

There are six basic price factors for diamonds:
Cut quality (proportions and finish)
Color
Clarity
Carat weight
Stone shape and cutting style
Treatment status (untreated or treated? type of treatment)

CUT QUALITY: (proportions and finish): This is a crucial factor which can affect prices by as much as 50%. The proportioning of the pavilion (bottom of the diamond) determines the overall brilliance of the stone. If the pavilion is too deep, the stone will look dark in the center; if it's too shallow, brilliance is diminished and a white circular area resembling a fisheye may be visible. In both cases light is leaking out of the pavilion instead of being reflected back to your eye.

If the crown (top of the diamond) is too shallow and the table (large top facet) is too large, the diamond will not have good sparkle and fire. **Fire** refers to flashes of rainbow colors.

If the crown is too high or the girdle (diamond edge) is too thick, the stone will look small for its weight and you'll pay for unnecessary weight that can reduce brilliance.

Look at figures 5.1 and 5.2 to see what a well-cut round diamond looks like face-up and from the side. Compare them to figures 5.3 to 5.6. For more photos and fuller information on judging cut, consult the *Diamond Ring Buying Guide* by Renée Newman and *Diamond Grading ABC* by Verena Pagel-Theisen.

Fig. 5.1 Well-cut diamond

Fig. 5.2 Profile of diamond in fig.

Fig. 5.3 A dark center resulting from a pavilion (bottom) that's too deep

Fig. 5.4 White circle (fisheye) cau by a pavilion which is too shallow

Fig. 5.5 A chunky marquise with a very thick girdle and a shallow, bulging pavilion, which decreases brilliance

Fig. 5.6 Thin crown. Deep pa ion. Face-up this diamond has duced fire, sparkle and brillian

Fig. 5.7 Diamonds of five different color grades ranging from D (colorless) to Z (light yellow). Actual colors are a little different than printed colors. *Photo and diamonds from J. Landau, Inc.*

Besides reading books that discuss diamond cut in more depth, you should also ask salespeople to show you examples of different cut qualities under magnification. Have them describe diamond proportioning in language you can understand. This is a good way to find out if a salesperson is able to help you select a well-cut diamond. You'll need assistance.

COLOR: Basically the less color the higher the price. Stones that are as clear as colorless water are the most expensive and have a D to E rating, D being the highest. As the letters descend towards Z, more color is present. See the GIA (Gemological Institute of America) color grading scale below.

D E F	**G H I J**	**K L M**	**N to Z**	**Z +**
colorless (white)	near colorless	faint yellow (top silver)	very light to light yellow	fancy yellow

Diamonds with a body color other than light yellow, light brown or light gray are called **fancy color diamonds**. These colored diamonds may cost a lot more than those which are colorless, especially if they're naturally red or blue. Some diamonds are colored artificially by irradiation or high-heat–high-temperature treatment.

CLARITY: The fewer and smaller the flaws, the higher the price. There are 11 GIA clarity grades. They are:

Fl: Flawless—no **inclusions** (flaws inside the diamond) and no **blemishes** (flaws on the surface). Rarely used in jewelry.

IF: **Internally Flawless**—no inclusions and only insignificant blemishes

Fig. 5.8 VS$_2$ radiant-cut (octagonal shape, brilliant cut) diamond

Fig. 5.9 SI$_1$ princess-cut diamond (square brilliant cut)

Fig. 5.10 A high SI$_2$

Fig. 5.11 A high I$_1$

Fig. 5.12 A low I$_2$

Fig. 5.13 I$_3$

VVS$_1$ & VVS$_2$: Very, very slightly included—minute inclusions difficult to see under 10-power magnification. Jewelers seldom keep these stones in stock.

VS$_1$ & VS$_2$: Very slightly included—minor inclusions ranging from difficult to somewhat easy to see under 10-power magnification. VS diamonds are available in jewelry stores.

SI$_1$ & SI$_2$: Slightly included, noticeable inclusions easy (SI$_1$) or very easy (SI$_2$) to see under 10-power magnification, but that normally aren't eye-visible.

I$_1$, I$_2$, & I$_3$: Imperfect—eye-visible inclusions face up that range from just visible (I$_1$) to extremely visible to the naked eye (I$_3$). Some I$_2$ and I$_3$ diamonds may be damaged by ultrasonic cleaning. They may also be less resistant to knocks.

CARAT WEIGHT: In most cases, the higher the carat weight category, the greater the per-carat price. A carat is a unit of weight equalling a fifth of a gram. The weight of small diamonds is often expressed in points. One point equals 0.01 carats.

There's a difference between the labels **1 ct TW** (one carat total weight) **and 1 ct** (the weight of one stone).

SHAPE & CUTTING STYLE: Some shapes such as rounds cost more than others like pear shapes. The effect of shape on price depends on the stone size, demand and available supply.

Radiants may cost slightly more than emerald cuts depending on size. They have the same shape but different faceting styles.

Patented and trademarked cutting styles typically sell for more than generic cuts of the same shape.

TREATMENT STATUS: Unlike colored gems, most diamonds are untreated. That could change. Before 1999, buyers only needed to know if diamonds were fracture-filled or laser drilled to improve their clarity, or irradiated to change their color.

In 1999, jewelry trade magazines announced that General Electric was able to turn a special class of brown diamonds colorless by heating them with high temperatures and high pressure (HTHP treatment). Brown diamonds typically sell for about 40%

to 75% less than colorless diamonds of the same quality and size. By the end of 1999, some of these HTHP-treated diamonds were being sold under the names of Pegasus, GE-POL, Monarch or the generic name "processed diamond." In 2000, a new name for them was introduced—"Bellataire."

Curiously, HTHP-treated diamonds are being sold in upscale stores. Even though jewelers buy them at about 15% less than untreated stones, some are able to sell them to customers at a premium by emphasizing their rarity. The customers probably don't know that jewelers wouldn't pay a premium for heat-treated diamonds and that these diamonds will become more common.

Don't let sales hype diminish your opinion of untreated diamonds. Gemstones which are naturally beautiful have historically been more highly valued than their treated counterparts.

Not all countries require disclosure of gem treatments, and some sellers don't comply with disclosure laws that exist. Therefore it's a good idea to **ask if a diamond you want is treated.**

Major sources: In 1998, Australia was the top diamond producer by *volume*, followed by DR Congo, Botswana and Russia. In terms of *value*, Botswana was the number one producer, followed by Russia, South Africa and Angola. These countries are still the leading sources. Namibia is also an important source. The most profitable diamond mine in the world is Jwaneng in Botswana.

Beware: Some sellers over-grade their stones and neglect to provide information about the quality of the cut. Their prices may seem low when in fact they might be higher than those of ethical jewelers. If you're buying an expensive diamond, either get one with a lab report from a respected lab or else make the sale contingent on an appraisal from an independent appraiser.

Many lab reports do not provide information about the proportioning of the bottom of the diamond (pavilion). That's one reason why you should examine stones before you buy them and deal with a seller who knows and cares about cut quality.

Diamonds that are fracture-filled, irradiated, drilled or heat & pressure treated should sell for less than untreated diamonds,

Fig. 5.14 Natural diamonds of high clarity and color. *Earrings and photo from Harry Winston, Inc.*

all other factors being equal. In addition, the fillings in fracture-filled diamonds might be damaged by repeated ultrasonic cleanings or by jewelry repair procedures involving direct heating.

The newest diamond imitation is synthetic moissanite. It reacts like diamond to thermal diamond testers, but jewelers can distinguish it from diamond because its facets appear doubled under magnification. Other imitation diamonds are easier to detect. For information and photos on identifying fake diamonds, consult the *Diamond Ring Buying Guide* by Renée Newman.

Care tips: Untreated diamonds without cracks and large inclusions can be cleaned by any method. You can soak them in soapy water, alcohol or an ammonia solution and then rub them clean with a lint free cloth. Ultrasonic cleaning is usually the easiest and most effective method. Most jewelers will clean your jewelry and check your diamond settings free of charge.

It's inevitable that you'll knock your hand and ring against furniture, counters and walls. If you're buying an everyday ring, select a mounting which protects the edge of your diamond from knocks and make sure the stone is securely set. A tension setting that leaves most of the girdle (edge) of the diamond exposed is not a wise choice for an everyday ring (fig.5.16). In addition, select a diamond that's free of serious cracks and that has a clarity no lower than I_1. Untreated diamonds with a good clarity can withstand hard wear.

Fig. 5.15 A diamond that's in good condition after 55 years of constant wear. The platinum ring setting prevented the edge of the diamond from being hit directly by hard surfaces.

Fig. 5.16 An impractical setting for an everyday ring because the edge of the diamond can come into direct contact with hard objects

You can obtain additional information on settings and jewelry craftsmanship from the *Gold & Platinum Jewelry Buying Guide: How to Judge, Buy, Test and Care for It* by Renée Newman.

6

Gems from Living Organisms

Pearls, amber, coral and ivory are not stones, but they're regarded as gems because they're attractive, relatively rare, and can be worn as jewelry. Instead of being faceted, they're usually polished, carved, or drilled. Of all the gems produced by living organisms, pearls are the best known and most highly valued.

Pearl Price Factors in a Nutshell

The following factors can affect the price of a pearl:

Luster
Pearl type (saltwater/freshwater, natural/cultured, whole/blister)
Thickness of the nacre (pearly substance secreted by mollusks)
Color
Shape
Size
Surface quality
Treatment status (untreated or treated? type of treatment)

LUSTER: Pearl brilliance; the shine and glow of a pearl. The higher and deeper the luster, the more valuable the pearl. Pearls with a high luster display strong and sharp light reflections and a good contrast between the bright and darker areas of the pearl. Pearls with low luster look milky, chalky and dull. Select pearls that have a good luster.

PEARL TYPE: Before you price a pearl, you should know, for example, if it's **saltwater** (from the oceans, sea, gulf or bay) or if it's **freshwater** (from a river, lake or pond). Good saltwater pearls (e.g., South Sea and Japanese akoya) can cost several times more than freshwater pearls of similar quality and size. One of the reasons for this is that one mussel in a lake can produce as many as forty freshwater pearls in one harvest. An oyster in the sea typically produces one or sometimes two saltwater pearls at a time.

It should be noted, however, that some new strands of large round pink freshwater pearls are retailing for over $10,000.

Fig. 6.1 Luster qualities ranging from high to very low

Fig. 6.2 Some Australian South Sea pearl colors

Fig. 6.3 Some Tahitian pearl colors

Fig. 6.4 Some South Sea pearl shapes: round, oval, drop, button, circled drop and baroque

Fig. 6.5 Surface qualities ranging from clean to heavily blemished

Natural pearls are more valuable than cultured pearls. **Natural pearls** are usually formed as the mollusk secretes layers of protective nacre (pronounced NAY-ker) around an irritant that *accidentally* enters the mollusk. The irritant can be a minute snail, worm, crab, or a particle of shell, clay or mud. **Cultured pearls** are formed around irritants that are *intentionally* introduced by man. The irritant may be a shell bead, another pearl or tissue from an oyster or mussel. The shape and size of the resulting pearls depends to a large degree on the shape and size of the implanted irritant.

Over 99% of the pearls on the market today are cultured. Perhaps the highest percentage of natural pearls sold today are found in Europe and the Middle East. In Europe, "pearl" means "natural pearl." In the United States, the term "pearl" has come to mean "cultured pearl" because natural pearls are not normally sold in jewelry stores. If a pearl is natural, it's usually called a natural pearl. According to the U.S. Federal Trade Commission, however, pearls that are cultured are supposed to be preceded by the word "cultured."

Whole pearls are much more valued than **blister pearls**—those which grow attached to the inner surface of a mollusk shell and **three-quarter pearls**—whole pearls that have been ground or sawed on one side, usually to remove blemishes. **Mabe pearls** are made from blister pearls by removing the interior, filling it with a paste and covering it with a mother of pearl backing. These assembled pearls offer a big look at a low price, but they're not as durable as non-assembled pearls.

NACRE THICKNESS: Nacre thickness is not a price factor for natural pearls because they're nearly all nacre. However, it is of critical importance in cultured saltwater pearls.

The thicker the nacre coating of a pearl, the better and more durable the pearl. Before about 1960, Japanese akoya pearl farmers left the pearls in the oyster for at least two and a half years. Around 1979, pearl harvesting started to be done just after six to eight months. The result—a lot of inexpensive, thin-nacre pearls on the market, many of which look like dull white beads and have nacre that's peeling off the pearls. Fortunately, better pearls with thicker nacre are also available, but they're rarely as thick as those cultured before the 1960's. South Sea pearls nor-

Fig. 6.6 Cultured freshwater pearl. *Brooch and photo from A & Z Pearls.*

Fig. 6.7 Cultured Japanese akoya pearls. *Pearls from A & Z Pearls; photo by John Parrish.*

mally have a thicker nacre coating than akoya pearls. Nacre thickness is one of the most important quality factors for cultured saltwater pearls because it affects both the beauty and durability of the pearls.

Nacre thickness is not as important a factor in cultured freshwater pearls as it is in saltwater pearls. This is because most freshwater pearls have no shell nucleus. When one is present, the nacre is usually thicker than in akoya pearls. One of the biggest selling points of cultured freshwater pearls is that they usually have a higher percentage of pearl nacre than their saltwater counterparts.

COLOR: Saltwater pearls that are yellowish usually sell for less than those which are white and light pink. Golden South Sea pearls from Indonesia and the Philippines are an exception and can sell for as much as white South Sea pearls, provided the gold color is intense and natural.

Natural-color black pearls (they're actually gray) can sell for as much as white pearls of the same size and quality, as long as they have overtone colors and are not just plain gray. The overtone colors, which are visible in the light-colored areas of black pearls, may be green, pink, blue or purple.

Pink overtones are desirable on white pearls and are visible in the dark areas of the pearl. Greenish or yellowish overtones tend to reduce the price of white pearls. Occasionally, iridescent rainbow-like colors are visible on pearls. Pearl iridescence is always considered a valuable quality.

The way in which color affects the pricing of freshwater pearls varies from one dealer to another. Often it has little or no effect. However, when comparing the prices of any pearls, try to compare pearls of the same type and color.

SHAPE: Normally, the more round and symmetrical the pearl, the more it costs. Unique, asymmetrical shapes, however, are also desirable, and are used to create distinctive pearl pieces. The lowest priced shapes are baroque (irregular and asymmetrical in shape) or have ring-like formations encircling the pearl.

SIZE: The larger the pearl the more it costs. An exception would be round pearls with a diameter of less than 7 millimeters. A 2–2½ mm strand, for example, might sell for the same price or

Fig. 6.8 Cultured mabe and blister pearls interspersed with rose quart tourmaline, chrysoprase and tanzanite cabs. *Gems from King's Ransom; pho to by Ron Fortier.*

Fig. 6.9 Cultured South Sea pearls. *Jewelry from Divina Pearls; photo by th designer, Christina Gregory.*

more than a 4–4½ mm strand (pearl measurements are generally rounded to the nearest half or whole millimeter). Pricing often depends on availability and demand.

SURFACE QUALITY: The fewer and smaller the flaws, the more valuable the pearl. Blemishes on single pearls tend to be more obvious and less acceptable than those on strands. It's normal for pearl strands to have some flaws.

Natural pearls normally have more flaws than cultured akoya pearls. That's because they've been in the oyster longer and have had more time to develop blemishes. Cultured pearls from the South Seas are also more likely to have flaws than akoyas, which have a thinner nacre coating.

TREATMENT STATUS: Dyed and irradiated pearls cost less than those of natural color. Irradiated pearls normally cost more than dyed pearls because the irradiation process is more costly and because it's usually reserved for higher quality pearls.

During the 1920's and 30's, however, dyed black pearls were considered fashionable and sometimes sold for as much as white pearls of similar size and quality.

Geographic sources: Japan is still the major producer of akoya pearls that are 7 mm and above in size. China has become a large producer of small akoya pearls. China is the main producer of freshwater pearls, but they're also cultured in the United States and Japan. Australia is the principal producer of white South Sea pearls, whereas Indonesia is the largest producer of golden South Sea pearls. A significant quantity of golden South Sea pearls are also produced in the Philippines. The majority of black pearls are cultured in Tahiti, but some are also produced in the Cook Islands and Mexico.

The highest percentage of natural saltwater pearls have been harvested in the Persian Gulf, the Red Sea and the Gulf of Manaar (between India and Sri Lanka). Natural freshwater pearls have been found in the rivers of the USA, Scotland, Ireland, France, Austria and Germany, but they're no longer commercially important.

Beware: Dyed and irradiated pearls are not always disclosed. For black and golden South Sea pearls that cost thousands of dollars, it's a good idea to get a report from a respected lab stating there's no evidence of artificial coloring, especially if you don't know the seller.

Imitation pearls are occasionally sold as cultured pearls. For information and photos on detecting fake and dyed pearls, consult the *Pearl Buying Guide* by Renée Newman.

A more common problem is pearls with nacre so thin it peels off. This can be detected both with the naked eye and a 10-power magnifier. You can usually avoid getting thin-nacre pearls by selecting pearls that have a high, rich luster. To learn how to evaluate luster, have salespeople show you a variety of luster qualities from very high to very low.

Care tips: Clean pearls by wiping them with a soft damp cloth after wearing them. Avoid ultrasonics, steam cleaners, detergents, bleaches, powdered cleansers, ammonia-based cleaners, and chemicals. Pearls are attacked by all acids, but it's safe to use acetone on pearls to remove glue and stains. Put your pearls on after applying hair spray, cosmetics and perfume. If you wear pearls often, have your jeweler check the strands about once a year to determine if they need restringing.

Amber

Amber is fossilized pine tree resin (sap). It was one of the earliest gems used for personal adornment. Of special interest to scientists are ambers containing insects, pollen, leaves and occasionally frogs and lizards that were trapped millions of years ago while the sap oozed out of pine trees. They provide a rare look at plant and insect life of that time period.

Most amber is brownish yellow to orange in color but it can also be blue, green or red. Brownish colors are the least valued. The best quality amber is transparent and either has no flaws or else has very distinctive inclusions.

Major deposits: The majority of gem quality amber is found along the Baltic coasts of Russia and Poland. Other significant sources are the Dominican Republic, Mexico, Myanmar, Sicily and Romania.

Beware: Amber is sometimes dyed to make it darker or a different color. The dye may fade.

Be on the lookout for **pressed amber** (also called reconstituted amber). It's made by heating small amber fragments and compressing them into larger pieces. It can be identified by magnification. A lot of natural amber is heated just to make it more transparent.

Amber can be separated from imitations such as plastic by placing it in a saturated salt solution. Amber will normally float whereas most imitations usually sink. One imitation that's harder to detect is copal, a recent fossil resin material from various trees such as the locust tree in South America.

Care tips: Amber scratches, abrades and melts easily. If it's left in the sun, it can dehydrate and crack. Avoid ultrasonics, all chemicals, brushes and heat. To clean amber, wipe it with a soft damp cloth; or clean it in cool soapy water, rinse and dry with a soft cloth.

Coral

Coral is formed by colonies of tiny boneless sea animals called coral polyps. They secrete a hard outer framework which becomes a coral home for them and which can eventually grow into reefs. The Mediterranean and Red Seas are the main sources of the finest coral. Much of it is fashioned and traded in Torre del Greco, Italy near Naples.

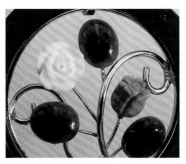

Fig. **6.10** Coral flowers and nephrite jade leaves

Coral occurs in a variety of colors—pink, red, orange, white, cream, black and occasionally blue or purple, but the most highly valued is red, followed by pink. The stronger and more even the color the better the quality. Coral is typically cut into cabochons, beads, cameos and figurines; or branch segments are drilled and strung into necklaces.

Major sources: Australia, Ireland, Japan, Malaysia, Western Mediterranean Sea, Philippines, Red Sea, Taiwan and Hawaii. Black coral is found in Australia, Hawaii and the West Indies.

Beware: Ask if the coral has been dyed to deepen or change the color. Dyed coral may fade and should cost less. Low quality material may be impregnated with glue-like material to fill and hide surface cavities, and broken pieces or cracks may be glued back together. Common imitations include bone, chalcedony, plastic, glass, and shell. Gilson coral is an imitation coral made by Gilson Inc.

Care tips: Coral scratches and abrades easily, and it dissolves in acidic substances such as vinegar and lemon juice. Avoid ultrasonics, all chemicals, brushes, bright light and heat. To clean coral, wipe it with a soft damp cloth.

Ivory

Ivory is dentine, a substance common to the teeth of all mammals. The term is used to refer mainly to elephant's tusks, but today ivory is also the teeth of hippopotamus, mammoth, narwhal, sea lion, walrus, whale and wild boar.

Since more and more ivory-bearing animals are threatened with extinction, trading in most new ivory has become illegal in much of the world. As a result, some new ivory pieces are dyed to make them appear as if they are valuable antiques. Today people are encouraged to use imitation ivory made from bone or palm nuts (vegetable ivory) as a substitute. Plastic is also used to imitate ivory.

Major Sources: Tanzania, Zaire. It's also found in India, Kenya, Senegal, Sri Lanka and Thailand.

Care tips: Ivory is soft and porous and it can shrink and discolor from heat. Avoid rough wear, ultrasonics, chemicals, brushes, bright lights and heat. To clean ivory, wipe it with a soft damp cloth; or clean it in soapy water, rinse and dry with a soft cloth.

7

Gold & Platinum Jewelry

J ewelry is normally made from **alloys**, mixtures of two or more metals. Gold, for example, is alloyed (combined) with metals such as silver, copper and zinc to make it harder, to change its color and/or to reduce its cost. Platinum alloys are usually made by combining platinum with ruthenium, iridium, palladium, cobalt or copper.

When comparing fine jewelry prices, find out the platinum or gold content of the metal. It's called **fineness**—the amount of gold or platinum in relation to 1000 parts. For example, gold with a fineness of 750 has 750 parts (75%) gold and 250 parts of other metals. An alloy containing 95% platinum has a fineness of 950.

In some countries, the **karat** is also used as a measure of gold purity. One karat is 1/24 pure, so 24 karat represents pure gold. Metal containing 75% pure gold is 18 karat (18K) gold. The table below lists karat qualities of gold jewelry.

Gold Content and Notation

Karatage	Parts Gold	Gold %	Fineness
24K	24/24	99.9%	999 or 1000
22K	22/24	91.6%	916 or 917
18K	18/24	75.0%	750
14K	14/24	58.3%	583 or 585
12K	12/24	50.0%	500
10K	10/24	41.6%	416 or 417
9K	9/24	37.5%	375

Fig. 7.1 Brooch of 18K rose gold set with a 13.5 mm Tahitian cultured pearl. *Handwoven by Barbara Berk; photo by Dana Davis.*

Platinum Content & Notation

Throughout the world, the purity of platinum is described only in terms of fineness. The markings, however, may vary slightly. In 1997, the U.S. Federal Trade Commission established the following guidelines for platinum markings:

♦ 950 parts or more per thousand of pure platinum can be marked "platinum" or "plat" without the use of qualifying statements.

♦ 850 to 950 parts per thousand can be marked in accordance with international standards of "950 Plat." or "950 Pt.," "900 Plat." or "900 Pt.," "850 Plat." or "850 Pt." Two- or four-letter abbreviations for platinum are permitted.

♦ less than 500 parts per thousand pure platinum cannot be marked with the word platinum or any abbreviation thereof.

In many European countries, platinum must have a purity of 95%. The typical markings are **Pt 950** or **950 Pt**. Occasionally, platinum chain products are made with 85% platinum and are marked Pt 850.

Other Jewelry Metal Terms

Budget-priced jewelry is made with the following metal types:

Gold filled (GF): Composed of a layer of gold mechanically bonded to a base metal using heat and pressure. In the United States, the layer must be at least 10K gold and 1/20th of the total weight of the object.

Gold overlay or rolled gold plate (RGP): Same as gold filled except the gold layer is thinner. It can be from 1/20th to 1/40th of the total weight of the object.

Gold electroplate (GEP:) Plating with a gold layer that is at least 7/1,000,000 of an inch thick. The object is dipped in a gold plating solution while an electrical current is used to bond the gold particles of the solution to the metal surface. The thickness of the gold depends upon the amount and duration of the current.

Sterling silver: Silver with a fineness of at least 925 (92.5%).

Vermeil: Sterling silver covered with at least 120/millionths of an inch of fine gold. The layer of gold may be either electroplated or mechanically bonded.

Gold versus Platinum

The natural beauty of gold, along with its workability, high value and history has made it the world's most important jewelry metal. Nevertheless, it's facing strong competition from platinum.

In the 1920's and 30's, platinum was the preferred metal for engagement and wedding rings in America and Europe. This was because platinum can be thin and dainty, yet sturdy, resistant to wear and better at securing stones than gold. Then in World War II, the U.S. government declared platinum a strategic metal and banned its use in all non-military applications, including jewelry.

Because of strong consumer preference for platinum's neutral color, white gold was substituted for platinum. White gold is created from yellow gold by adding metals such as copper, zinc, silver and/or palladium. After the embargo was lifted, platinum

Fig. 7.2 An ensemble of platinum jewelry by Siegfried Becker. *Photo from Platinum Guild International USA.*

did not regain its previous popularity in America because white gold was less expensive and easier to work with, and the public accepted it.

Platinum is again becoming the metal of choice for settings and wedding and engagement rings. Consumers are discovering that most platinum alloys are harder, denser and more durable than 14K and 18K gold. In addition, the white metal compliments diamonds that are colorless. Unlike white gold, it does not need to be plated with rhodium to look white.

There are also advantages to gold jewelry. Gold earrings and necklaces are more comfortable because they're lighter in weight than platinum if they're the same style. Gold has a distinctive yellow color, it costs less, and more jewelers are trained to work with it. Gold compliments the skin tone of some people more than white metals.

Geographic sources: In 1999, South Africa was the largest producer of gold, followed in descending order by the United States, Australia, Canada, China, Indonesia, Russia and Peru.

Approximately 70% of the world's platinum is mined in South Africa, 20% in Russia, 6% in North America and the rest elsewhere.

Beware: Plated gold is sometimes sold as genuine gold, so beware of street vendors and of prices that seem too good to be true. Some fake gold can be detected with a magnet. Unlike many fakes, gold is not magnetic. Fineness stamps on clasps can be misleading. For example, it is legal for a 14K clasp to be attached to a fake gold chain with a jump ring that is bent closed, provided it is not soldered or welded to the chain.

Nonetheless, fineness stamps are helpful. Therefore select jewelry that is stamped. Look for the stamp on the inside of the piece and on the clasp. You may need a hand magnifier to read it.

Fig. 7.3 Fineness stamp for 95% platinum and 18K (750) gold next to trademark for Varna Platinum.

The stamp doesn't guarantee the purity, but it's a good indication. Preferably there should be a trademark stamped next to the fineness mark. This may enable authorities to track the maker of the piece if the metal is different than stamped.

Don't expect consumer protection laws to be as strict in developing countries as they are in industrialized countries. When buying jewelry abroad, it's especially important to deal with jewelers that meet the criteria discussed in Chapter 12.

Care tips: Clean gold and platinum with soapy water and a soft cloth. Avoid using brushes because they can scratch gold and platinum. Ammonia solutions and jewelry cleaners may also be used provided the jewelry is not set with stones such as pearls, coral, emeralds, malachite and turquoise, which may be damaged by cleaning solutions.

Avoid cleaning jewelry with toothpaste, powder cleansers or scouring pads because these can wear away the metal. If jewelry is so dirty that it can't be cleaned with ammonia or soapy water, have it cleaned professionally. Some jewelers do this free of charge.

Avoid wearing gold jewelry in swimming pools or hot tubs that have chlorine disinfectants, and never soak it or clean it with bleach. The chlorine can pit and dissolve the metals with which the gold is alloyed, causing prongs to snap and mountings to break apart. Chlorine does not affect pure gold or platinum.

For further information and photos on alloys, metals testing and markings, read the *Gold & Platinum Jewelry Buying Guide: How to Judge, Buy, Test & Care for It,* by Renée Newman.

8

Jewelry Craftsmanship

If you want your jewelry to last and to hold gems securely, pay attention to the mounting and setting. Here are some basic tips:

Mountings:

♦ **Select sturdy mountings for everyday rings and bracelets.** Rings that are wire thin and bracelets that can bend and dent do not last long. Platinum mountings can normally be thinner and more delicate than those made of gold. This is because platinum is stronger and more dense than most gold alloys.

♦ **Avoid hollow rings and chains.** They provide a big look at a low price, but they're hard to repair and they're less durable than solid jewelry. Rings, bracelets, and chains need to be more durable than earrings, brooches and pendants, which are not subjected to as much wear and tear.

♦ **Check to see if the piece is well-finished on the back and underneath.** If it is, chances are it's well constructed. If it's rough, or has excess solder, holes and an illegible fineness stamp, this suggests the piece was done quickly without much care. It's helpful to use a hand magnifier when checking a jewelry piece.

 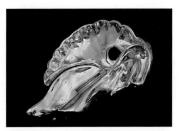

Fig. 8.1 An unacceptable rough finish on the back of a cast brooch

Fig. 8.2 A high quality finish on the back of a cast brooch

♦ **Make sure the clasp works** if there is one. It may be defective or hard to open. Ask the salesperson to show you how to open and close it. Then try it twice yourself. For bracelets, see if you can open and close them with one hand.

Fig. 8.3 Safety catch with a knob small that it doesn't stay closed

♦ **Ask if the jewelry is well crafted** and find out why it is or isn't. Jewelers that sell well-made pieces often like to explain why their mountings, settings and finishes are better than those of competitors. You can learn a lot about workmanship by listening to them. Salespeople must understand jewelry craftsmanship in order to help you select a well-made piece,

Settings

♦ **Determine if there's enough metal holding the stone.** Use a ten-power hand magnifier. For example, if prongs are missing, the stone is not secure.

♦ If possible, **make sure the edge of the stone is flat against the seat** (the groove in the metal which supports the stone). There shouldn't be space between the prongs and the stone.

Fig. 8.4 Improperly set stone. Note the space between the stone and the prong on the right.

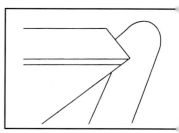

Fig. 8.5 Edge of stone flat against the seat in the prong

♦ **Verify that you can see most of the stone.** Gems shouldn't be covered by so much metal you can hardly see them. No more than one-third of the stone should be covered.

♦ For every-day prong-style rings, **get hand fabricated or die-struck (machine made) settings.** They're stronger than cast settings, which are more porous and brittle. Ideally, the settings will be made of platinum, because it's stronger and wears better.

♦ **Ask your jeweler to show you some examples of good-quality setting** so you'll have a basis for comparison.

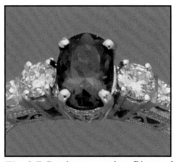

g. 8.6 Bulky irregular prongs

Fig. 8.7 Good prong setting. *Ring and photo from Varna Platinum.*

♦ **Check jewelry for loose stones by shaking or tapping it lightly** with your forefinger while holding it next to your ear. If you hear the stones rattle or click, there's a problem.

♦ **Make sure pearls are secured to jewelry with a metal post and not just glued to the mounting.** Otherwise they can easily be knocked out of the mounting. Ideally the post should screw into the pearl. Even if the glue fails, the screw will still hold the pearl securely.

For more information on jewelry craftsmanship, finishes, chains and settings consult the *Gold & Platinum Jewelry Buying Guide: How to Judge, Buy, Test & Care for It,* by Renée Newman.

Fig. 9.1 Chinese freshwater pearls from King's Ransom. *Photo by Ron Fortier.*

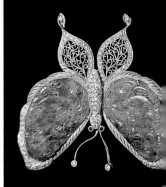

Fig. 9.2 Burmese jadeite brooch f[...] Mason-Kay. *Photo by Don Kay.*

Fig. 9.3 Untreated Nigerian red tourmaline

Fig. 9.4 Montana moss agate

Fig. 9.5 Tanzanite from Tanzania

Fig. 9.6 Rainbow moonstone fro[...] India

9

Notable Gem Sources

Listed below are the primary sources of the gems discussed in this book along with those of precious metals. Other deposits are included in the write-ups of each gem under "Major sources."

AFRICA

Botswana:	diamond
DR Congo:	diamond, malachite
Egypt:	formerly the most important source of peridot
Kenya:	aquamarine, grossular garnet, rhodolite, ruby, spessartine garnet, tsavorite
Madagascar:	agate, morganite, blue sapphire, pink sapphire, spodumene, yellow beryl
Namibia:	blue chalcedony, blue & blue-green tourmaline
Nigeria:	aquamarine, red tourmaline, spessartine garnet
Republic of Mali:	grandite (Mali garnet)
Tanzania:	chrome tourmaline, color-change garnet, iolite, malaya garnet, rhodolite garnet, ruby, fancy-color sapphire, tanzanite, tsavorite
South Africa:	diamond, gold, hydrogrossular, platinum, pyrope, tiger's-eye
Zambia:	amethyst, aquamarine, emerald

ASIA

Afghanistan:	lapis lazuli, red topaz, tourmaline (bicolor, blue-green and pink)
Cambodia:	sapphire, zircon
China:	aquamarine, pearls (akoya and freshwater), nephrite jade, peridot, tourmaline, turquoise
Hong Kong:	a shopper's paradise for all gems and jewelry even though none are mined there
India:	agate, almandine garnet, bloodstone, chalcedony, iolite, moonstone, quartz cat's-eye, star ruby; a cutting center for lower-quality diamonds

Fig. 9.7 Mexican fire opal carved by Sherris Cottier Shank. *18K S-Curve Brooch handwoven by Barbara Berk; photographed by Robert Weldon; photo courtesy* Professional Jeweler.

Fig. 9.8 Australian boulder o[

Indonesia:	South Sea pearls (golden)
Japan:	coral, pearls
Kashmir:	former important source of the highest quality sapphire

Myanmar (formerly Burma): jadeite jade, moonstone, peridot, ruby, sapphire, spinel

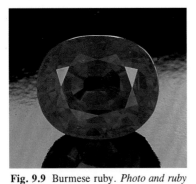

Fig. 9.9 Burmese ruby. *Photo and ruby from Fred Mouawad.*

Fig. 9.10 Colombian emerald

Pakistan:	aquamarine, emerald, kunzite, peridot, pink topaz, tourmaline
Singapore:	a shopper's paradise for all gems and jewelry even though no gems are mined there
Sri Lanka (formerly Ceylon):	alexandrite, cat's-eye (chrysoberyl), garnet, moonstone, padparadscha, ruby, sapphire (blue & fancy-color), zircon; cutting center for colored gems
Taiwan:	cutting center for colored gems
Thailand:	ruby, sapphire, zircon; a trading and cutting center for colored gems, especially ruby and sapphire

EUROPE

Belgium:	**Antwerp:** a cutting and trading center for diamonds
Germany:	**Idar-Oberstein:** a major cutting center for colored gemstones and processing center for agate
Italy:	gold manufacturing center; **Torre del Greco:** a trading center for coral
Poland:	amber
Scotland:	smoky quartz
Russia:	alexandrite, amber, demantoid garnet, diamond, yellow beryl
Ukraine	blue topaz, bicolor topaz

NEAR & MIDDLE EAST

Iran:	turquoise
Israel:	a cutting and trading center for diamonds

NORTH AMERICA

Canada:	**British Columbia:** nephrite jade, hessonite garnet **Newfoundland:** labradorite
USA:	gold **Western United States:** agate, chalcedony, jasper **Arkansas:** clear quartz **Arizona:** fire agate, peridot, petrified wood, pyrope garnet, turquoise

California: abalone pearls, benitoite, pink & red tourmaline, flawless bicolor tourmaline
Hawaii: black coral, peridot from volcanos for tourists
Montana: sapphire (blue and fancy color)
Oregon: sunstone
Utah: red beryl
Wyoming: black jade

Mexico: agate, chrysocolla, fire agate, yellow labradorite, fire opal, pink grossular (rosolite), turquoise; **Taxco**, a silver manufacturing center

SOUTH AMERICA

Bolivia: ametrine
Brazil: agate, alexandrite, amethyst, aquamarine, cat's-eye (chrysoberyl), citrine, emerald, iolite, morganite, quartz cat's-eye, rose quartz, sard, spessartine garnet, spodumene, topaz, tourmaline, yellow beryl
Chile: lapis lazuli
Colombia: emerald
Uruguay: agate, amethyst

SOUTH PACIFIC

Australia: black jade, diamond, gold, opal, sapphire, South Sea pearls
Lightning Ridge, New South Wales: black opal
Queensland: boulder opal, chrysoprase, sapphire, yowah opal
South Australia: light opal, Andamooka matrix opal
Western Australia: diamond, sapphire, South Sea pearls
French Polynesia: black pearls (Tahitian pearls)
New Zealand: abalone mabe pearls, nephrite jade

10

Euphemisms, Marketing Terms & Misnomers

What does the term **"clarity enhanced diamond"** mean to you? I asked several lay people this question. Nobody knew exactly what it was. The most common response was "I don't know" or "I have no idea, what is it?." Here are other responses:

♦ "They did something to the diamond to make it look better."
♦ "It means the color is clearer and brighter, so it's more expensive."
♦ "The diamond is fake."
♦ "It sounds like a low-quality diamond that was pumped up."
♦ "It's a better quality diamond than others."
♦ "It's a doctored-up diamond."
♦ "It doesn't mean anything. How can you enhance a diamond? It's either clear or it isn't."

Sellers may tell you that a clarity enhanced diamond is one whose imperfections have been eliminated thanks to amazing achievements in modern technology.

In actuality, "Clarity enhanced diamond" is a marketing term for **fracture-filled diamonds**—diamonds whose fractures have been masked with a thin glass-like film. Although you may not see the fractures, they're still present. "Clarity enhanced" can also refer to **diamonds that have been laser drilled** to remove black flaws by bleaching them and sometimes filling them. Both of these treated diamonds are worth less than untreated diamonds of similar size and quality, they're harder to resell, the treatment is not always permanent, and some jewelry repairs involving heat (e.g. retipping) can damage the filler. Nevertheless, clarity-enhanced diamonds can be an affordable alternative for people who want a big look at a lower price.

It's not surprising that suppliers of fracture-filled diamonds prefer to describe them as clarity enhanced. This allows them to disclose the treatment in a positive, vague manner. However, sellers to the general public should explain the meaning of "clarity-enhanced" to their customers because lay people don't know what it means. The term even misleads some people into thinking that the enhanced diamond is more valuable than an untreated diamond. Gem laboratories should define "clarity-enhanced" on their lab documents or else they should use clear, specific terminology such as "fracture-filled." Otherwise they're not providing proper disclosure.

Gem colors are often described with non-color adjectives such as champagne, honey, pistachio, grape, cornflower and sherry. These marketing terms are ideal for displays and advertisements because they evoke positive images that entice you to buy. However, they're not appropriate for lab reports, appraisals and serious gemological texts since they don't give you a good visual idea of gem color. For example, depending on whom you talk to, sherry-colored topaz is either yellow, orange, brownish yellow or reddish. That's because people have different opinions as to what is the color of sherry. Consequently an insurance appraisal which describes a topaz as sherry-colored won't be very helpful if the owner needs to replace a lost or stolen topaz.

Within the diamond industry, the term "champagne" is a euphemism for light brown. Since the presence of brown and gray in gems often lowers their value, dealers prefer to avoid these two color terms when describing gems and even metals. For example, platinum has an attractive gray color, but it's described as a white metal. If it were really white, platinum would look like plastic.

When used to describe colored gems, "champagne" is typically an ambiguous marketing term. "Champagne garnet," for example, has been used to refer to light yellow, light pink, light orange and light brown garnet.

Salespeople that have your interests at heart will explain trade euphemisms and marketing terms to you clearly. But since many sellers are more interested in making a quick sale than in establishing a long-term relationship of trust, you may need to refer to the following table:

Table 10.1: Trade euphemisms translated into clear English

B-jade	Jade that's been bleached and impregnated with a synthetic filler
C-jade	Jade that's been dyed in addition to being bleached and impregnated in some cases
Champagne diamonds	Light brown diamonds
Cognac diamonds	Brown diamonds
Clarity enhanced diamond	Usually means fracture-filled diamond. Can also mean laser drilled.
Clarity enhanced emerald	Fracture-filled emerald. The filling may be oil, wax, natural resin and/or an epoxy-like substance. Almost all emeralds are fracture filled.
Clarity enhanced ruby	Ruby with glassy residues in fractures as a result of being heat treated in a flux such as borax. "Clarity enhanced" can also denote rubies that are oiled or cavity filled.
Created	Synthetic, lab-grown, man-made
Enhancement	Treatment
Faux pearls	Imitation pearls
Feather	Crack, fissure, fracture of any size
Processed diamond	Heat and pressure treated diamond
Stabilized	Impregnated with a colorless bonding agent such as plastic
Thermal enhancement	Heat treatment

Misnomers

Sometimes gems are sold under names that misrepresent the true identity. These names are called misnomers. For example, garnet may be called an "American ruby" or "Cape ruby" to make seem more valuable. If a salesperson adds a qualifying word or pref to a gem name, ask him or her to explain what it means. Som misnomers are:

Ceylon diamond	zircon
Brazilian diamond	colorless topaz
Herkimer diamond	quartz
Mogok diamond	topaz
Evening emerald	peridot
Medina emerald	green glass
Oriental emerald	green sapphire
Spanish emerald	green glass
Soudé emerald	green doublet
African jade	translucent green garnet
Amazon jade	amazonite
Australian jade	chrysoprase
Colorado jade	amazonite
Indian jade	aventurine quartz
Pikes Peak jade	amazonite
Oregon jade	dark green jasper
Swiss jade	dyed chalcedony
German lapis	dyed blue jasper
Swiss lapis	dyed blue jasper

Black onyx	dyed chalcedo
Majorica pearl	imitation pear
Red Sea pearls	coral beads
Semi-cultured pearl	imitation pear
Balas ruby	spinel
Bohemian ruby	rose quartz
Brazilian ruby	topaz
California ruby	garnet
Colorado ruby	garnet
Cultured ruby	synthetic ruby
Siberian ruby	tourmaline
Spinel ruby	spinel
Brazilian sapphire	tourmaline or topaz
Meru sapphire	tanzanite
Oriental sapphire	chrysoberyl
Spinel sapphire	spinel
Water sapphire	iolite
Topaz	citrine quartz
Madeira topaz	citrine quartz
Smoky topaz	smoky quartz
Spanish topaz	citrine quartz

11

Having Jewelry Custom Made

I f you don't find the type of jewelry you're looking for, you may wish to have it custom made. Many Asian countries are noted for their fast service—often 1 to 2 days. They can be this quick because they have more jewelers per capita than countries such as the United States. A jeweler in Asia may have only one or two pieces to work on at a time, whereas one in the USA may be handling 30 or 40 jobs at once. When having jewelry custom made, follow the guidelines below:

♦ Try on jewelry pieces that resemble what you want. What looks good in a picture may not look or feel good on you.

♦ If possible, have good drawings, photos or models of the jewelry piece you want made. Never assume that the jeweler understands your verbal description of what you want. Be as specific as possible about how you want the jewelry to look.

♦ Don't assume a piece of jewelry will look exactly as it does in a photo. It should, however, have a close resemblance. The best way to get exactly what you want is to have a model or sample.

♦ If you have a ring that fits well and has about the same band width as a custom ring you are ordering, show it to the salesperson or jeweler so they can choose the best ring size for you. The sample metal rings they have you try on can sometimes suggest the wrong size.

♦ Always tell a jeweler you need the ring earlier than you actually do, especially if it's a complicated job. In Asia, you should allow 3 or 4 hours extra; and in countries such as the United States, at least 3 or 4 days. Either the jewelers may not finish on time, or alterations may be needed.

Work out an acceptable delivery date and have it put in writing. But still be prepared for delays. It's best not to rush custom-made jewelry.

♦ If possible, avoid having jewelry custom made in December in countries that celebrate Christmas. Since jewelers are rushed and overworked at that time of year, they might not do their best work then.

♦ Get a written estimate of the cost of the jewelry. If more stones are needed than estimated, the jeweler is not expected to give them to you free of charge. He should, however, get your permission before doing anything that would increase the estimated cost of the jewelry.

♦ If you supply the gemstones for custom-made jewelry, find out in advance who will be responsible if your stones are lost or damaged during setting or recutting. The jeweler is not always liable if something unfortunate happens to them. Reliable jewelers, however, will either feel morally obligated to replace damaged or lost stones or else will clearly warn you that your stones are at risk.

♦ Make sure that gold and platinum pieces are stamped with the fineness. A manufacturer's trademark is also desirable.

♦ Know the refund policy of the jeweler. It is normal for jewelers to retain at least a portion of your deposit if you decide not to buy the ring you ordered, particularly if it's a style that would be difficult to sell. Pay deposits with credit cards. If the store does not deliver the job as promised, it will be easier to get your money back.

When you have a piece custom made, it often means more to you than ready-made jewelry. The piece is unique, and you played a role in creating it. The experience of having jewelry made should be a positive one. Prevent it from turning into a negative one by taking the necessary precautions.

12

Choosing a Jeweler

When you choose a jeweler or salesperson, here are some things you should consider.

Are they knowledgeable? Do they know how to evaluate gem and jewelry quality? Are they well-informed about gem treatments? The more informed salespeople are, the more capable they are of helping you make wise choices that fit your needs.

Someone in the store should have gemological credentials such as those listed in the chapter on appraising. It's important, for example, that at least one staff member be able to detect synthetic stones. Even honest jewelers may end up selling synthetics as natural stones if they're unable to identify them.

Are they candid and ethical? Do they tell you both the good and bad points of their inventory? Do they disclose gem treatments without your having to ask? Do they explain quality and treatments in clear language, or do they just rely on trade euphemisms and marketing terms? Jewelers that are upfront with information demonstrate they care about you.

Do they have a love for gems and jewelry? If so, they probably know about new trends and developments in the industry, and they can probably help you select unique, appropriate jewelry for yourself and others. They can also help you appreciate it more. Jewelers who only care about price and weight are not likely to have well-crafted, artistic designs.

How to Determine if a Seller is Knowledgeable and Candid

Jewelry industry brochures usually tell you to choose a jeweler by getting recommendations, by checking credentials and length of experience and by finding out if they're affiliated with trade organizations. This is good information, but it's not adequate.

Just because a jeweler is a member of trade organizations and has diplomas displayed on the wall does not guarantee he or she is ethical and well-informed. Conversely, some of the most knowledgeable people in the industry do not have gemology diplomas. In addition, it's easy to lie about your experience and educational background.

Getting recommendations from someone you trust is not always easy or possible, especially when you're traveling abroad. More often than not, you'll need to judge for yourself if a jeweler is reliable. To make a good judgment, you'll need to know some basics so that you'll be able to understand and assess the salespeople. Reading this book is a good start. You should then be prepared to ask some of the following questions:

1. Could you tell me something about this piece (or stone)? A salesperson who can compare it to other pieces and who can tell you about the background and quality shows more expertise than one who can only tell you the price, the weight and the identity of the metal and stone(s) by reading the tag.

2. Which one of these pieces (stones or strands) is more valuable and why? Two of the advantages of buying jewelry in a store rather than from a catalogue or the internet is that you get to see the merchandise before buying it and you get the free services of a jewelry consultant, provided the seller is knowledgeable. When a jeweler can explain quality differences to you, this indicates he's a more competent consultant and he's probably a better buyer of merchandise for his store than a jeweler who can't.

3. Are these stones treated (and point to the stones of your choice)? If sellers tell you that none of their emeralds, for example, are treated in any way, this is a strong indication they're either ill-informed or dishonest. Review the information in Chapter 2 on treatments so you'll know how and what stones are enhanced. If sellers tell you that an individual stone is not treated ask how they know it's not treated and ask if they're willing to write this on the receipt. Untreated stones can be worth more than those that aren't.

The way in which jewelers disclose treatments is one of the best indications of how ethical they are.

4. Can you tell me something about the cut of this stone? It's not sufficient for a salesperson to simply describe the shape of a stone and to tell you it's a fine make, if it is. You need specific information about why it's a fine, average or poor make. For example, they should be able to point out if a stone has a strong window, a very thick girdle, a unique faceting design, etc. You could also ask the salesperson to show you one of the best-cut gemstones in the store and to compare it to an inferior one. Not only will you learn more about cut, you'll also learn if you're dealing with a knowledgeable salesperson. Keep in mind, that rubies, sapphires and emeralds are normally not as well proportioned as most diamonds.

5. How would you rate the quality of your jewelry craftsmanship. Why? Jewelers that sell well-made jewelry often like the opportunity to explain why their mountings, settings and finishes are better than those of competitors. You can learn a lot about workmanship by listening to them. Salespeople must know something about jewelry craftsmanship in order to help you select a well-made piece,

6. Will you show me the piece (or stone) under magnification? If they aren't willing to provide you with a loupe (hand magnifier) or a microscope, consider shopping elsewhere.

7. Are you willing to put in writing what you've told me verbally about the piece (stones)? Reliable jewelers will say yes.

8. What's your return policy? It's a good sign when jewelers back up their merchandise and claims by a 100% money back guarantee. Some jewelers only allow exchanges in order to prevent customers from "borrowing" their merchandise for special events. When you buy jewelry away from home, though, exchanges become impractical. There are many jewelers throughout the world who offer a 100% money-back guarantee on jewelry that is not custom made. It's best to deal with one of them.

When buying expensive jewelry abroad, have the salesperson give you a written copy of their return policy or have them write it on the receipt. Then pay by credit card, not a bank debit card. If there's a problem with the piece when you get back home, it will be easier to get your money back.

13

Making the Purchase

General Guidelines:

The preceding chapters gave tips on selecting gemstones and jewelers. Here are some additional guidelines:

♦ **When buying abroad, ask if the store has an outlet in your home country** that can service you and make refunds. If it does, get the name, address and phone number.

♦ **Know how much the purchase is in your home currency.** Foreign currency prices can be confusing.

♦ **Have verbal agreements put in writing.** For example, have them write on the receipt or give you a written copy of their "money-back guarantee" policy. If a store is doing custom work, have them write the delivery date on the receipt.

♦ **Consider having expensive gems checked by a qualified lab in the city of purchase.** It's easier to return goods and get your money back on the spot than thousands of miles away. Be wary if a store is overly pushy about using a specific appraiser. They may be working together.

♦ **Get a detailed receipt.** The receipt should at least include:
1. the identity and shape of the stone(s),
2. the identity and purity of the metal
3. the carat weight of any major stones and the total weight of any smaller stones of each gem type
4. the millimeter dimensions of loose stones

This information will help identify the stone or jewelry later on. For added protection, have the store specify if the stone is of natural origin on the receipt. In the United States, it's against the law to call a synthetic ruby simply a ruby. The gem name must be qualified with terms such as "synthetic" or "lab-grown." Not all countries have laws like this.

If the store tells you a gem is untreated, have them write this on the receipt too. Then it won't be your word against theirs if the stone turns out to be treated. Many countries do not have treatment disclosure laws.

♦ **Ask the store to make a photocopy of the receipt** or give you a duplicate, especially if it's a large purchase. You can keep one in your wallet and another with your purchase, or else you can mail one copy home in case the other is lost or stolen. When you return from your trip you'll need two copies anyway—one to keep at home and one for your safe deposit box.

♦ **Ask the salesperson to give you his or her business card** with the store's phone number, street address, and fax number (if they have one). You may need to contact them later.

♦ **If you bought jewelry at a store a tour director recommended, get his or her address and phone number.** Tour directors can be a big help if problems arise later on.

♦ **Pay with a credit card whenever possible.** Resist a bargain for cash on large purchases. Credit card companies can be an excellent source of protection if and when problems arise.

When traveling to countries with a lot of poverty, you should notify your credit card company(s) and ask if there will be any problems using their card. A Canadian friend of mine was advised by her travel agent to do this when she went to Mexico, but she forgot to call the card company. When she tried to buy some silver jewelry in Taxco with her credit card, the stores couldn't get an authorization. Yet her Mexican hotels were able to get an authorization number for her card.

My friend had no problems buying jewelry in Taxco with a debit card. Debit cards aren't the same as credit cards and there are distinct disadvantages to using debit cards, which I'll discuss in the next section. If a store can't or won't accept your credit cards, think twice before making a major purchase from them.

It's advisable to travel with at least two credit cards. If you become ill or injured, or have to return home early for family reasons, you'll probably need to use them.

Credit Cards Versus Debit Cards

It was easier for my friend to use her debit card in Mexico because it didn't offer her as much protection as a credit card. Some basic differences between the two cards are:

♦ **Credit card users have full access to their money** in the event of card theft, fraud or a dispute about a charge. They don't have to pay until the dispute is settled, which may take a few months. **Debit card holders must wait to be reimbursed for unauthorized debits.**

♦ **Standard credit cards offer consumers a free loan until the due date of payment.** Meanwhile, your money can be earning interest in an interest-bearing account. An exception to this is the so called "secured" card, used by people with bad credit, which charges user fees.

When you use a debit card, your account is immediately debited.

♦ **In case of loss or theft, credit cards offer more protection.** Merchants must get an authorization number to avoid responsibility for purchases made on stolen credit cards. This isn't true of debit cards, which is why many merchants in the U.S. no longer require pin numbers or ID's for debit cards.

♦ **Many credit cards offer you protection from fraudulent merchants.** Using a debit card is almost like paying cash.

♦ **Credit cards provide better documentation for purchases.** You have a record of when and where a purchase was made. It's easy to find unauthorized charges when you review your credit card statement.

If you forget to enter a debit card purchase in your check book, you can end up overdrawing on your checking account. In addition, it's hard to prove duplicate charges and overcharges when you use a debit card.

Many banks in the U.S. are reissuing ATM bank cards that can also be used as debit cards. The disadvantage is that these new ATM cards can be used in some stores without a pin number. If your ATM card is also a debit card and you'd prefer to have it be a cash card that can only be accessed with your pin number, simply ask your bank to downgrade it to just an ATM card.

American banks may lead you to believe that unauthorized debits are inconsequential by saying the most you can lose is $50 or $500, provided you notify them of lost or stolen debit cards.

Here's what banks don't normally tell you.

♦ You probably won't have access to any money stolen from your checking account until after the dispute is settled.

♦ Your checks can bounce and it can take months to correct your credit record if someone uses your debit card fraudulently.

♦ Your checking account is no longer safe to use as long as someone else has access to your debit card.

In November 1999, I learned firsthand what a nightmare unauthorized debits can be. A company unknown to me debited my checking account for $1000 by giving my bank the wrong account number. Even though it was obvious from computer records that my account was erroneously debited, the bank didn't want to return my $1000 until they were reimbursed from the firm that debited my account. After a month of phone calls and bank visits, the bank finally decided to give me provisional credit for $1000. I learned later that I should have received my money within two weeks of filing the dispute notice. The moral of the story is do whatever you can to avoid unauthorized debits and keep as little money as possible in your checking account.

Should you ever have a problem in America with unauthorized debits of your bank account, you can find out your legal rights by looking up Regulation E on www.bankinfo.com.

When Problems Arise

If an appraiser or gem lab tells you your purchase abroad is either overpriced or misrepresented, proceed as follows:

♦ First send the store a photocopy of the appraisal or lab report (by fax or air mail), and explain how you would like the matter resolved. It's a good idea to follow up with a phone call. You should let the store have a chance to give you an explanation. Appraisers are not infallible, nor are they all highly qualified. In fact, some have little experience valuing and identifying some of the colored gems mined abroad.

♦ If the store ignores you or refuses to resolve the matter, tell the owner or manager that you will be filing formal complaints with business and trade organizations in his city and with your credit card company (if you paid by credit card). If the store still refuses to cooperate, then follow through on your threats.

♦ To get the addresses of business and jewelry organizations, try calling the trade commissioner that represents the country where you made the purchase. Explain the problem, and ask if he can help you. You can usually get the phone number of the trade commissioner by calling the local consulate. Two organizations that handle complaints about jewelers in the United States and Canada are:

Jeweler's Vigilance Committee
25 W. 45th #400, New York, NY 10036,
(212) 997-2002, www.jvclegal.org

Jeweler's Vigilance Canada, Inc.
27 Queen St. E. #600, Toronto, ON M5C 2M6, Canada
(416) 368-4840

♦ If you paid by credit card, phone the credit company within 30 days if possible, explain the problem, and ask them to stop payment on your purchase. They'll tell you if they need documentation and let you know how to return the merchandise. Get the name of the person on the phone and the file or reference number of the case (if one can be assigned).

♦ If you bought the jewelry from a store a tour director recommended, you may want to contact him or her first. Good tour directors can save you a lot of time and hassle if problems arise. They will contact the jeweler for you, explain the problem, and relay your requests. Either the jeweler or tour director or both will get back to you to take care of the matter.

♦ If you bought the jewelry from a store recommended in a brochure of a reliable tour operator in your country, contact the tour company. They will give the jeweler one of two choices—either resolve the matter or lose all future business from them.

♦ When you return merchandise, it's best to send it insured registered air-mail and to pay for a return receipt, whenever possible. You may need proof that you returned the merchandise. Sometimes the insurance offered is not adequate to cover the amount of the purchase. You may be able to get more insurance if you send it express mail. It's hardest to get insurance for packages sent to developing countries. This is another reason you should be careful when making large purchases abroad.

If you plan on making a major jewelry purchase while traveling, find out in advance how much insurance your postal service offers to the countries where you might buy jewelry. **If there's no way for you to safely return merchandise via insured mail, you could end up being stuck with misrepresented goods.** As mentioned earlier, some stores abroad may have offices in your home country where you can return jewelry. This is the ideal alternative.

♦ Keep originals of all documentation regarding your case. Only send copies.

It's best to avoid problems before they occur. Learn about gems before you buy; review the tips in this and the preceding chapters; and be wary of deals that seem to good to be true. Every seller needs to make a profit, even those abroad.

14

Choosing an Appraiser

I f you were buying a classic car, you wouldn't go to the seller's mechanic to have the car checked. You'd take it to your own. Likewise, when you're buying expensive jewelry, you shouldn't just rely on documents provided by the seller. You should have it evaluated by an appraiser who is an unbiased third party and who has your interests in mind. Appraisals paid for by sellers are not independent appraisals.

Four reasons for getting an independent jewelry appraisal are:

♦ To verify the identity and quality of the gems and metals used.
♦ To get additional information about treatments, origin, and quality that the seller may not have known.
♦ To have a written third-party document that will be recognized by insurance companies. Many insurance companies do not recognize appraisals provided by the seller.
♦ To determine if you paid a fair price. It's best to find this out from a professional appraiser who doesn't sell jewelry. Competing jewelers may downgrade and under-appraise the merchandise so they can afterwards sell you something else.

In addition, sellers may have a tendency to give inflated appraisals. This can result in unnecessarily high insurance premiums. For most insurance policies in the United States, the insurance company has the option of replacing your merchandise or paying you cash for the amount it would cost them to replace it, whichever is lower; don't expect to get cash for the value listed on an inflated appraisal.

However, you don't want an undervalued appraisal either. There have been some cases where the insurance coverage has been voided by the company because of either undervalued or highly inflated appraisals. Obtain a legitimate appraisal from a qualified independent appraiser and avoid paying more than what you need to in premiums to the insurance company.

The purpose of most appraisals is to obtain insurance coverage. An insurance appraisal states the value of replacing a piece; it doesn't establish what you can gain in selling the piece. The type of appraisal that gives you the immediate cash value of your jewelry is called a liquidation appraisal. If you're only interested in a verbal estimate of how much you can sell a piece for, you can usually find that out for free. Just go to some jewelers or dealers and ask them what they'll pay for the piece. But be aware that the price they offer you can be lower than what you might obtain in a more competitive active market such as auction.

How to Find a Qualified Independent Appraiser

Some ways to find appraisers are:

♦ Get recommendations from friends and jewelers
♦ Look at the phone book and internet listings under appraisers: However, many of the listings will be for real estate appraisers and some of the jewelry appraisers may be unqualified or may just want to buy your jewelry or sell you something.
♦ The best way to find an appraiser is to call, write, fax or e-mail an appraisal organization and ask for the names of qualified members in your area. Some organizations that will give you names of independent appraisers are listed below and on the next page:

In the USA

Accredited Gemologists Association (AGA)
3309 Juanita Street, San Diego, CA 92105
Phone (619) 286-1603 FAX (619) 286-7541

American Society of Appraisers (ASA)
Box 17265, Washington, D.C. 20041
Phone (703) 478-2228 FAX (703) 742-8471

International Society of Appraisers (ISA)
16040 Christensen Road Suite 102 Seattle, WA 98188-2929
Phone (206) 241-0359 FAX (206) 241-0436

National Association of Jewelry Appraisers (NAJA)
P.O. Box 6558, Annapolis, Maryland 21401-0558
Phone (301) 261-8270

Canada

Canadian Jeweller's Institute
27 Queen St. East Toronto, Ontario M5C 2M6 Canada
Phone (416) 368-7616 ext 223   FAX (416) 386-1986

Great Britain

National Association of Goldsmiths NAG
78a Luke Street
London EC2A 4XG, England
Phone 44 207 613-4445   FAX 44 207 613-4450
E-mail   NAG@jewellersuk.com

Australia

Jewellery & Allied Trades Valuers Council
New South Wales, Australia
Phone 02 9267 1927   FAX 02 9267 1928

Jeweller Valuers Council of Queensland
Queensland, Australia
Phone 07 3221 1782   FAX 07 3221 1156

Council of Jewellery Appraisers
South Australia, Australia
Phone 08 8300 0182   FAX 08 8300 0001

Australian Jewellery Valuers Council
Tasmania, Australia
Phone 03 6331 7880   FAX 03 6331 3488

NCJV Inc., Victoria, Australia
Phone 03 9621 2439   FAX 03 9629 2904

NCJV Inc., Western Australia, Australia
Phone and FAX   08 9409 2009

After you get the names of some appraisers, you'll need to interview them to find out if they're qualified to appraise your jewelry. When interviewing an appraiser you should ask:

♦ What are your qualifications?
♦ How much do you charge?
♦ What does your appraisal fee include?

Qualifications to Look For

To appraise gems, you need to know how to identify gems and gem treatments. Competent professional appraisers should have one of the following gemological diplomas to prove they've gained the required education needed to identify gemstones.

- ◆ **FGA**, Fellow of the Gemmological Association of Great Britain
- ◆ **FCGmA**, Fellow of the Canadian Gemmological Association
- ◆ **GG**, Graduate Gemologist (Awarded by the Gemological Institute of America)
- ◆ A gemologist diploma from another school or association, equivalent in stature to those listed above.

The FGA, FCGmA and GG are known internationally. No matter where you travel in the world, you'll be able to find jewelry professionals holding these diplomas.

Although the gemologist diplomas listed above are important, they don't in themselves qualify people to be appraisers. Appraisers must also be skilled in valuation theory; they must be familiar with gem prices, jewelry manufacturing costs, and the legal aspects of appraising. Appraisers must have trade experience, integrity, and the initiative to keep up with the market and new developments in valuation theory and gemology.

This means appraisers should have taken appraisal courses and performed appraisal work after getting their gemologist diplomas. Some of the titles awarded to appraisers in the United States are:

- ◆ **CAPP**, Certified Appraiser of Personal Property. This is the highest award offered by the International Society of Appraisers. To receive it, one must attend their appraisal courses and pass exams. Trade experience is a prerequisite.

- ◆ **CGA**, Certified Gemologist Appraiser. This is awarded by the American Gem Society to certified gemologists that pass their written and practical appraisal exam. Trade experience is a prerequisite.

- ◆ **CMA**, Certified Master Appraiser. This is the highest award offered by the National Association of Jewelry Appraisers. To receive it, one must take the NAJA appraisal studies course, pass a comprehensive theory and practical appraisal examination, and have a NAJA or AGA Certified Gem Laboratory.

◆ **MGA**, Master Gemologist Appraiser. This is the highest award offered by the American Society of Appraisers. To receive it, a person must pass their appraisal tests and have a gemologist diploma, an accredited gem lab, and at least 3 to 5 years appraisal experience.

Besides telling you about their educational background and titles, appraisers should also discuss their experience and the type of jewelry and gems they usually appraise.

Appraisal Fees

As a consumer, you have the right to know in advance the approximate cost of an appraisal. Occasionally, an appraiser will tell a caller that it's unethical or unprofessional to quote prices over the phone. This isn't true. Professional appraisers should at least be able to tell you their hourly fee and/or their minimum charge if they have one. Some will tell you a flat or approximate appraisal charge for the piece when you describe it to them over the phone. However, in fairness to the appraiser, they are entitled to change their estimate upon seeing the piece if you have played down certain areas of difficulty or have not described it fully.

There are some people that will offer to appraise your jewelry free of charge, even if you haven't bought it from them. This is a sign that either they want to buy the jewelry from you or else they want to lure you into their store to sell you some of their merchandise. Professionals charge for their services, whether they be lawyers, doctors, accountants or appraisers.

Appraisal fees are charged in a variety of ways. Some are listed below:

◆ A flat fee per item, sometimes a lower fee for each additional piece brought in at the same time
◆ An hourly rate (often combined with a minimum fee)
◆ A rate fully or partly based on the gemstone type
◆ A rate based on the type of report you're seeking, based on the degree of work required.

♦ A percentage rate of the appraised value of your jewelry. The higher the value, the more money the appraiser earns. If you want an appraisal that is as objective as possible, avoid appraisers with this type of fee structure. This is an unethical fee if the appraiser is a member of any of the associations listed previously. The Internal Revenue Service doesn't recognize appraisals done by people who charge percentage fees.

What Does the Insurance Appraisal Include?

The key service the appraiser will provide to you is an accurate, detailed, word picture of the item you're having appraised. The structure of the resulting report will tell you something about the quality of the appraiser's work, and it will help you to better compare appraisal fees. It's understandable that a five-page report with a photo will cost more than one with only a two-sentence description and an appraised value, and you should avoid the latter type. Items that professional independent appraisers normally include with their reports are:

♦ The identity of the stone(s) and metal(s)
♦ The measurements and estimated weights of the stones. (If you can tell appraisers the exact weight of the stones, this will help them give you a more accurate appraisal. Therefore, when buying jewelry, ask stores to write on the receipt any stone weights listed on the sales tags).
♦ Relevant treatment information
♦ A description of the color, clarity, transparency, shape, cutting style, and cut quality of the stones. The grading and color reference system used should also be indicated. Appraisers use different color communication systems to denote color. Four of the best known ones are GemDialogue, AGL Color/Scan, GIA GemSet and Munsell.
♦ Plots of the inclusions in the stones (of either all or only the major stones)
♦ A test of the fineness of the metals
♦ Approximate weight and description of the mounting
♦ The name(s) of the manufacturers or designers of the piece when this is known
♦ A cleaning and inspection of the piece

♦ A photograph
♦ A list of the tests performed and the instruments used.
♦ Definitions or explanations of the terminology used on the report
♦ A biographical sketch of the appraiser's credentials
♦ A Certification of Appraisal Practices sheet (a written code of business ethics for appraisers)

On rare occasions, a country of origin report may also be included, but this requires a high level of expertise.

Suppose you ask someone what their appraisal fee includes and they start specifying a few of the items above. Then suppose you ask someone else and they reply, "The value and a description of the piece. What more do you expect?" Haven't those two answers helped you determine who is more qualified to appraise your jewelry?

Besides knowing what appraisers' fees include, you should know what their appraisals look like. Have them show you a sample, and check it for thoroughness and professionalism.

Appraising Jewelry While you Wait

Not all appraisers have a policy of appraising jewelry while you wait. However, it may be inconvenient for you to make two separate trips for an appraisal—one to drop off the jewelry and one to pick it up. Most appraisers will try to accommodate your needs. Some appraisers will only appraise it in front of you. However, they often send you the final written appraisal afterwards. No matter what their policy, you usually need to make an appointment.

Even if it doesn't matter to you whether you leave the jewelry with them or not, it's not a bad idea to ask appraisers if they do on-the-spot appraisals. Their answers will give you added information about them. For example, look at the four responses on the next page. These are actual answers to the question, "Can you do the appraisal on the spot?"

♦ "Only if you pay double because it will keep us off the floor away from selling."

♦ "Yes, but my schedule is limited. What I mostly do is custom design, not appraising."
♦ "Yes, but it will have to be in the afternoon. I reserve mornings for jewelers and their questions and appraisals."
♦ "No, I need time to analyze the quality of your gemstones and metal work and to do research to arrive at a probative value."

Which of the four are probably most qualified to appraise a $9000 sapphire ring? Which of the four might be most qualified to appraise custom designed gold jewelry? Which are most likely to give an unbiased appraisal?

Jewelry appraising is an art. There's a lot more to it than simply placing a dollar value on a stone or jewelry piece. If your jewelry has a great deal of monetary value, it's important that you have a detailed, accurate appraisal of it. Take as much care in selecting your appraiser as you did with your jewelry.

15

Gem Lab Documents

For gems that cost several thousand dollars, it's a good idea to get two types of documents—an independent appraisal describing and evaluating the stone, and a lab report from a major gem laboratory.

Lab reports don't tell you what a stone is worth. They identify the stone and the treatments it may have undergone. They may also indicate its geographic origin and/or evaluate its quality.

Perhaps you're wondering why you'd need a lab report when appraisals also provide identification, treatment and quality information. Major laboratories have greater expertise, more sophisticated equipment and more opportunities to examine important gems than the average jeweler or appraiser. As a result, they're better equipped to detect enhancements and synthetic gems, and their documents usually carry more weight than appraisals when gems are bought and sold. If you plan to sell an expensive gem on the international market or through an auction house such as Christie's or Sotheby's, it should be accompanied by a report from an internationally recognized lab.

Some stores provide lab reports with their stones. These are helpful aids, especially when buying gems abroad; but for a stone such as a $20,000 emerald, you should obtain your own lab report at the time of purchase. Get a written promise of a 100% refund if you're not satisfied with the results of the report. Changes may have occurred in the emerald fillings since the store got the lab report, and the fillers might therefore be easier to identify. Also, the stone could have been treated after the report was issued.

If you're only spending a few hundred dollars on a gemstone, it's not financially worthwhile to get a lab report. A good appraisal will do.

Listed below are some of the most respected gem laboratories in the world along with the types of reports they offer. They all provide treatment reports so these aren't indicated. "**ID**" stands for "identification report," "**origin**" stands for "geographic origin report."

AGL (American Gemological Laboratories, Inc.)
580 Fifth Ave. Suite 706, New York, NY 10036
phone (212) 704-0727 Fax (212) 764-7614
Colored stone ID, origin, & quality; diamond grading

AGTA Gem Testing Center
18 E. 48th Street, Suite 1002, New York, NY 10017
phone (212) 752-1717 Fax (212) 750-0930
Colored stone ID & origin; pearl ID

AIGS (Asian Institute of Gemological Sciences)
Jewelry Trade Center, 6th floor, 919 Silom Road
Bangkok 10500, Thailand
Phone (662) 267-4325/7 Fax (662) 267-4327.
Colored stone ID, origin, & quality; pearl ID; diamond grading

American Gem Society Laboratory (only for the trade)
8881 W. Sahara Ave., Las Vegas, NV 89117
Phone (702) 255-6500 Fax (702) 255-7420
Diamond grading

C.C.I.P. Gemological Laboratory (C.C.I.P. Service Public du Contrôle des Diamants, Perles Fines et Pierres Précieuses)
2 Place de la Bourse, 75002 Paris, France
Phone (33-1) 40 26 25 45 Fax (33-1) 40 26 06 75
Colored stone ID & origin; pearl ID; diamond grading

Deutsch Diamant und Edelstein Laboratorien Idar-Oberstein
(German Diamond and Gemstone Laboratories Idar-Oberstein)
Mainzer Str. 34, D-55743 Idar-Oberstein, Germany
phone 49-6781-981355 Fax 49-6781-981357
www.gemcertificate.com Email: info@gemcertificate.com
Colored stone ID & origin; pearl ID; diamond grading

GAGTL (Gemmological Association and Gem Testing Laboratory of Great Britain) 27 Greville Street, London EC1N 8TN, UK phone 44 (207) 404-3334 Fax 44 (207) 404-8843.
E-mail: gagtl@btinternet.com
Colored stone ID & origin; pearl ID; diamond grading

GIA (Gemological Institute of America) **Gem Trade Laboratory Inc.**, 5355 Armada Drive, Carlsbad, CA 92008
phone (800) 421-7250 & (760) 603-4500 or
580 Fifth Ave., New York, NY 10036, (212) 221-5858
   Colored stone ID; pearl ID; diamond grading

Gübelin Gem Lab Ltd (GGL),
Maihofstrasse 102, CH-6000 Lucerne 9 / Switzerland
phone (41) 41 429 1717, Fax (41) 41 429 1734
   Colored stone ID & origin; pearl ID; diamond grading

SSEF (Swiss Gemmological Institute)
Falknerstrasse 9, CH-4001, Basel, Switzerland
phone (41) 61 262-0640   Fax (41) 61 262-0641
   Colored stone ID & origin; pearl ID; diamond grading

How Lab Reports are Sometimes Misused

When used properly, gem lab reports can be a big help to buyers. They serve as a documented second opinion by impartial experts (when issued by reputable labs). Unfortunately, they are sometimes misused in the following ways:

♦ A lab report may be used with an inferior stone of the same weight. In other words, the document doesn't match the stone. A con artist can have a good stone certified more than once and then use the extra reports for other stones of the same size.

Avoid ripoffs like this by dealing with reliable jewelers and by examining stones carefully before you buy them.

♦ A synthetic stone may be cut to match a gemstone on a report. Then it's substituted for the natural stone.

♦ A stone may be treated after a report is issued stating it's not treated.

♦ An identification report from a respected lab may be used to make a very low quality stone seem valuable. If a stone, for example, is identified as a natural ruby on a report, this does not mean it's worth a lot. You should see a quality analysis of the stone before you make a judgment.

♦ Occasionally the grades on a document may be altered. Most labs make it very difficult to change or counterfeit their documents. Consequently, this is seldom a problem. If you have a question about a report, you can verify the information on it by calling the lab that issued it.

♦ Quality-analysis reports from non-existent labs may be used to mislead buyers. The grades on these reports are often inflated. Before relying on information from a lab report, check out the lab. Interview them on the phone about their qualifications and the type of research they conduct. Ask for references and find out if reputable jewelers, auction houses and gemological organizations know about them and use them.

Tips on Using Lab Reports

In order to gain maximum benefit from these lab reports and at the same time avoid their pitfalls, keep in mind the following suggestions:

♦ **Don't buy gems solely on the basis of a lab report.** Always examine the stones yourself with and without magnification before you buy them. Occasionally, the stone may be different than the one on the report, or a stone might have been damaged since the report was issued.

Nevertheless, it's far better to buy an expensive gemstone with a lab report from a respected lab than to buy one without a report, especially when buying gems abroad.

♦ **Don't buy gems in sealed plastic containers which you are not allowed to open.** Clear plastic covers can mask gem flaws and cutting defects. People involved in gem scams often sell sealed stones with a written warning such as "Breaking the seal will invalidate all guarantees." Legitimate dealers will allow you to look at the stone outside of its packet or container.

♦ **Don't buy expensive jewelry and gems through the mail or over the phone or internet if you don't know the seller.** These are probably the most common situations in which lab documents are misused.

♦ **Avoid gem investment schemes even when the stones come with lab reports.** People have lost their life savings by believing promises of high returns on gem investments. If a stone is merely identified as a natural ruby or sapphire, this does not necessarily mean it is valuable. Its quality must be taken into consideration.

Keep in mind too, that some appraisers give stones inflated values on their reports, even when they note quality characteristics. This may be due to lack of experience, inadequate training or collusion with sellers.

♦ **Remember that lab documents are not infallible.** They only represent the opinions of the labs issuing them. That's why reputable gem laboratories never guarantee their reports.

♦ **Keep in mind that a written report cannot give a complete picture of a gem**. You have to see the stone to really know what it looks like. Lab reports were never created to be a substitute for viewing a stone. Use them as an aid to judging quality and as a confirmation that a stone is real and natural. But when it's time to make the final choice, you be the judge.

On the next five pages are documents from five gemological labs whose reports are used on the international market by dealers and auction houses. These labs are also noted for their research and contributions to the field of gemology.

American Gemological Laboratories ™

580 Fifth Avenue
Suite 706
New York, N.Y. 10036
Tel: (212) 704-0727
Fax: (212) 764-7614

Gemstone Buyer's Report ™

DOCUMENT NO: CS 00000 (SAMPLE)

DATE: 15 March, 2000

The information contained in this report represents the opinion of American Gemological Laboratories regarding the characteristics of the colored stone(s) submitted for examination. The conclusions expressed are American Gemological Laboratories' interpretation of the results obtained from gemological instruments and grading techniques designed for this purpose. Conclusions may vary, within reasonable tolerances, due to the subjective nature of colored stone analysis.

IDENTIFICATION: Natural Emerald, Colombian.*

SHAPE AND CUT: Emerald Cut

CARAT WEIGHT: 5.320 Cts.

MEASUREMENTS: 12.25 x 10.12 x 6.58 mm.

COLOR GRADE: 4.5 / 70*

Color Rating/Tone   4 - 5 / 70

Color Scan $G_{95} B_{20} Y_{15}$

Light Source   Duro-Test: Vita Lite

CLARITY GRADE: Mo_2*

Texture   Faint

CUTTING GRADE: Good (4)

Depth %   65.0%

Brilliancy Range   50 - 70%

Brilliancy Average   60 - 70%

FINISH GRADE: Very Good - Good (3 - 4)

CLARITY ENHANCEMENT INFORMATION: *

Type   Organic: Polymer Type
Arthur Groom Gematrat™ Process

Degree   Moderate

Estimated ESI   Enhancement Stability Index™
High (Exc. - Very Good: 7 - 8)
Consumer Reference (Estimated)

COMMENTS:

*Total Quality Integration Rating: Very Good. "Based on available gemological information, it is the opinion of the Laboratory that the origin of this material would be classified as Colombia. "The image contained in this document is for representational purposes only and is not necessarily actual color or size. "The conclusions expressed in this report are based on Laboratory determinations effective as of the completion date of this analysis (17 March 2000).

This report prepared by:

AGL

Digital Image Enlarged For Detail

Digital Ultra Violet Tracer Image™

	0 5 10 15 20 25	30	35 40 45 50	55	60	65 70 75	80	85 90 95 100	
	V. Light	Light	Light-Med.	Medium		Medium - Dark		Dark-V. Dark	
Tone (AGL) (0 = Colorless, 100 = Black)									

	1	2	3	4	5	6	7	8	9	10
	Excellent	Very Good		Good		Fair			Poor	
Color Rating (AGL)										

Sample emerald report from American Gemological Laboratories

1239090

The Gem Testing Laboratory
of Great Britain

SAMPLE

GEM TESTING REPORT

Examined by X-radiography, a single-row graduated necklace of sixty five 'pearls'. The largest 'pearl' varies in width from approximately 11.5 mm. to 11.6 mm. and the smallest from approximately 7.0 mm. to 7.2 mm. in width.

Weight of necklace = 75.0 grams.

Extensive samples were found to be **NATURAL PEARLS.**

N.B. This type of examination does not allow for every 'pearl' in the necklace to be identified. The 'pearls' must be removed from the 'silk' for every 'pearl' to be determined.

The Gem Testing Laboratory of Great Britain is the official CIBJO recognised Laboratory for Great Britain

Only the original report with signatures and embossed stamp is a valid identification document.
This report is issued subject to the conditions printed overleaf.

The Gem Testing Laboratory of Great Britain

GAGTL, 27 Greville Street,
London, ECIN 8SU, Great Britain

Telephone: +44 171 405 3351
Fax: +44 171 831 9479

SAMPLE

Signed _____
Alan J. Clark FGA DGA

Signed _____
S.J. Kennedy FGA DGA

Date _____
25th May 2000

Sample pearl report from the Gem Testing Laboratory of Great Britain

GIA
GEM TRADE LABORATORY

New York Headquarters
580 Fifth Avenue | New York, NY 10036-4794
T: 212-221-5858 | F: 212-575-3095

Carlsbad
5355 Armada Drive | Carlsbad, CA 92008-4699
T: 760-603-4500 | F: 760-603-1814

DIAMOND GRADING REPORT

January 03, 2000

73846302

Laser Inscription Registry	GIA 10012345
Shape and Cutting Style	ROUND BRILLIANT
Measurements	6.90 - 6.97 x 4.20 mm
Weight	1.25 carat

Proportions

Depth	60.6 %
Table	61 %
Girdle	MEDIUM TO SLIGHTLY THICK, FACETED
Culet	VERY SMALL

Finish

Polish	VERY GOOD
Symmetry	VERY GOOD
Clarity Grade	VS1
Color Grade	F
Fluorescence	NONE

Comments:
Sample Sample Sample Sample Sample

This Report is not a guarantee, valuation or appraisal. This Report contains only the characteristics of the diamond described herein after it has been graded, tested, examined and analyzed by GIA Gem Trade Laboratory under 10X magnification, and/or has been inscribed, using the techniques and equipment available to GIA Gem Trade Laboratory at the time of the examination and/or at the time of being inscribed, including fully corrected triplet loupe and binocular microscope, master color comparison diamonds, standardized viewing environment and light source, electronic carat balance, synthetic diamond screening device, high intensity short wave fluorescence imaging system, short wave ultraviolet transmission detection system, optical measuring device, micro laser inscribing device, ProportionScope™, ultraviolet lamps, millimeter gauge, and ancillary instruments as necessary. Red symbols denote internal characteristics (inclusions). Green or black symbols denote external characteristics (blemishes). Diagram is an approximate representation of the diamond, and symbols shown indicate type, position, and approximate size of clarity characteristics. All clarity characteristics may not be shown. Details of finish are not shown. The recipient of this Report may wish to consult a credentialed Jeweler or Gemologist about the importance and interrelationship of cut, color, clarity and carat weight.

KEY TO SYMBOLS
· Crystal
⌐ Feather
· Pinpoint
∧ Natural

Sample diamond report from the GIA Gem Trade Laboratory

GÜBELIN
GEM LAB

EDELSTEIN-BERICHT · RAPPORT DE PIERRE PRECIEUSE
GEMSTONE REPORT

No. **SPECIMEN**
Datum · Date 8 May 2000

Gegenstand · Objet · Item One faceted gemstone

Gewicht · Poids · Weight **25.43 ct**

Schliff · Taille · Cut
Form · Forme · Shape cushion-shape
Stil · Style · Style brilliant cut / step cut
Abmessungen · Dimensions · Measurements 17.24 x 13.85 x 10.98 mm

Transparenz · Transparence · Transparency transparent

Farbe · Couleur · Colour **blue**

IDENTIFIKATION · IDENTIFICATION

Spezies · Espèce · Species
NATURAL CORUNDUM

Varietät · Variété · Variety
SAPPHIRE

Gemmological testing revealed characteristics
consistent with those of sapphires originating from:

Burma (Myanmar)

Bemerkungen · Commentaires · Comments No indications of thermal enhancement (NTE).

Sapphires which have not been enhanced by
heat are scarce.

GEMMOLOGISCHES LABOR · LABORATOIRE GEMMOLOGIQUE · GEMMOLOGICAL LABORATORY
Maihofstrasse 102 · CH-6000 Lucerne 9 · Switzerland · Tel. (41) 41 - 429 17 17 · Fax (41) 41 - 429 17 34
www.gubelinlab.com · e-mail: gubelinlab@compuserve.com

G. Bosshart, M. Sc. SFIT, G.G. Christopher P. Smith, G.G.

Wichtige Anmerkungen und Einschränkungen auf der Rückseite · Remarques au verso · Important notes and limitations on the reverse.
Copyright © 1999 Gübelin Gem Lab Ltd.

Sample sapphire report from the Gübelin Gemmological Laboratory

Gemstone Report
Expertise de pierre précieuse
Edelstein-Expertise

No. 00000

Weight / Poids / Gewicht

3.978 ct

Cut / Taille / Schliff

antique cushion, brilliant / step cut

Measurements / Dimensions / Masse

9.09 x 8.24 x 5.89 mm

Colour / Couleur / Farbe

red of strong saturation

IDENTIFICATION / IDENTIFIKATION

TREATED RUBY

Comments / Commentaires /
Bemerkungen

The analysed properties confirm
the authenticity of this transparent ruby.

With evidence of thermal enhancement and
artificial glassy residues in voids and fissures.
Extent of enhancement: moderate

Origin: Burma (Myanmar)

SSEF

Basel, 18 March 1998

Swiss Gemmological Institute
Institut Suisse de Gemmologie
Schweizerisches Gemmologisches Institut

SPECIMEN

magnification 1.5 x

Dr. L. Kiefert, FGA

Prof. Dr. H.A. Hänni, FGA

Sample ruby report from the Swiss Gemmological Institute

16

Customs

Common Regulations

Whenever you enter a foreign country, your belongings are subject to search. Here are some of the items customs officials throughout the world are looking for:

♦ **Drugs**. Even legitimate drugs may be confiscated, so be sure your medications are in their original labeled bottles and just take the amount you'll need while traveling. Also carry a copy of your drug prescriptions or a written statement from your doctor saying you need the medication(s).

♦ **Weapons and ammunition**. Leave them at home.

♦ **Endangered species**. Don't travel with ivory jewelry or accessories made from animals such as sea turtles, whales, rare reptiles, mammals and birds. They could be confiscated.

♦ **Commercial quantities of goods**. If you're carrying merchandise destined for another country, declare it anyway at intermediary ports of entry and have good proof as to where you're taking the goods. Otherwise you could be charged duty and/or fined for not declaring them.

♦ **Agricultural products and plants**. Flowers, plants, meat products, fish, dairy products and fresh fruits & vegetables may be seized to help prevent the country from being infested with unusual insects and microorganisms. Australia, New Zealand and the USA are particularly strict. Even airline food, sack lunches, and some canned foods may be confiscated.

♦ **Counterfeit products.** Normally no counterfeit copyrighted goods such as copies of videos or computer programs are allowed under any circumstances. The United States does allow one article of each type of product that bears a protected trademark, such as a designer handbag if it's for personal use.

Duty Free Goods and Exemptions

Customs duties are levied in your home country and in countries where you're leaving gifts or commercial goods. Some people think that if they buy goods in a duty free shop, they won't have to pay duty on them or declare them when they return to their home country. This is false.

"**Duty free**" simply means that items don't have import duties or taxes included in their price. For example, whisky bought in a duty free store at the Singapore airport does not have Singapore duties included in the price. However it's subject to duty when you arrive home, and it must be declared. If you're traveling with more than the permitted amount of liquor, you could even be charged duty or have it confiscated when you just travel through a country with it.

Incidentally, jewelry sold in duty-free shops is not necessarily cheaper than elsewhere. In fact, often the opposite is true because the shops at the airport have little or no competition.

At the end of this chapter, you'll learn how you can get customs information on the internet for specific countries. Duties, exemptions and restrictions vary depending upon the country. Most countries publish customs pamphlets you can pick up at consulates or airports. "Know Before You Go" is a good one for the USA.

In the United States, there's a **$400** exemption for items bought for your personal use provided you haven't used the exemption within the preceding 30-day period. The goods must accompany you on your return, and your stay abroad must have been at least 48 hours, except if you're returning from Mexico or the U.S. Virgin Islands.

The duty-free exemption is **$600** for items bought in 24 countries in the Caribbean basin and **$1200** if they're from U. S. Insular possessions—Guam, American Samoa and the U.S. Virgin Islands. These exemptions amounts are subject to change and may be different when you read this book.

There is a flat duty rate of 10% on the first $1000 worth of purchases above the personal exemption. Above that amount, duty percentages are based on the item and the country of origin and manufacture. Fine art, antiques over 100 years old and many items from developing countries may be exempt from tax. Loose gemstones are usually duty free in the USA. Duty rates can be complex. For example, duty percentages on watches vary depending on the number of jewels, the type of case, the price, and the type of movement and display.

The personal exemption in Australia is also $400 but Australian dollars are worth less than U.S. dollars and the Australian exemption does not include liquor and tobacco allowances.

In July 1999, the 7-day duty- and tax-free personal exemption for Canadian residents was increased from CAN$500 to CAN$750 including liquor and tobacco allowances.

The New Zealand accompanied goods exemption is NZ$700 excluding the liquor and tobacco allowance.

In the UK, £175 is the personal customs allowance on goods from outside the European Union. This excludes the liquor, tobacco and perfume allowance.

The last section of this chapter tells you how you can find much more detailed customs information about these and other countries on the internet. All exemptions are subject to change.

U.S. Duty Rates on Jewelry and Gems

When you shop for gems abroad, it's helpful to know in advance how much duty you'll have to pay on them. Duties are listed in the *Harmonized Tariff Schedule of the United States* (HTSUSA), which you should be able to find at your local library. This schedule is also included as part of the *U.S. Customs House Guide*. An internet address that lists U.S. duties and import information is:

www.dataweb.usitc.gov/scripts/tariff2000.asp

Type in the product category and click on "list items."

Duties vary depending on the country of origin of the goods. Duty-free or reduced-rate tariffs apply to countries classified as **GSP (Generalized System of Preferences)** or that have made special trade agreements with the United States. GSP countries are underdeveloped countries that have good trade relations with the US. Most countries in South America, Central America, Africa, Southeast Asia, Eastern Europe and the Middle East are GSP countries. Japan, Singapore, Hong Kong, Canada and Western Europe are categorized as developed countries and are **not** GSP.

Most jewelry bought in GSP countries is duty free. There are exceptions. Normal duty tariffs are levied on gem-set jewelry from Thailand and on precious metal jewelry from India, Turkey and the Dominican Republic.

The U.S. has special trade agreements with Canada, Mexico and Israel which exempts many goods made in these countries from duties. Jewelry is one of these duty-free items.

If countries do not have Normal Trade Relations (NTR) status with the US, goods bought there are either prohibited or have a higher than normal tariff rate. Listed below are countries which are **non-NTR** countries (formerly called **non-MFN**, Most Favored Nation):

Afghanistan	North Korea
Cuba	Vietnam
Laos	Yugoslavia (Serbia & Montenegro)

The countries below have conditional restoration of normal trade relations and are subject to disapproval semiannually or annually by joint resolution of Congress. All but Albania are former Soviet Union republics.

Belarus	Moldova
Albania	Russian Federation
Armenia	Tajikistan
Azerbaijan	Turkmenistan
Georgia	Ukraine
Kazakhstan	Uzbekistan
Kyrgyzstan	

n	Duty rates for NTR countries	Rates for non-NTR countries
set diamonds	0%	0%
set precious and semi-pre-us stones	0%	10%
ded semiprecious stones ng temporarily	2.1%	50%
tural and cultured pearls, ded and temporarily strung	0%	10%
ss imitation pearls and rl beads, not strung and set	4%	60%
ral	2.1%	10%
velry articles of precious or niprecious stones, valued over $40 per piece	3.3%	80%
velry articles of precious or niprecious stones, valued er $40 per piece	6.5%	80%
velry articles of natural rls	3.3%	80%
velry articles of cultured rls	5.5%	110%
ecious metal (o/than silver) icles of jewelry and parts reof	5.5%	80%
cklaces and neck chains of d	range from ≈5% to 5.8%	80%

Duty rates are designed to protect the commercial interests of a country. Since there are a lot of American jewelry manufacturers, the United States levies duties on jewelry made abroad to encourage people to buy jewelry locally. However, gem-quality diamonds, rubies and emeralds are not mined in the U.S., so there's no need to impose duties on them.

You may have heard stories about diamond smugglers. It would be stupid to smuggle loose diamonds bought abroad into the U.S. because there's no duty on them. Normally, if you declare loose gemstones, you don't pay duty. However, if you don't declare them and get caught, you could have them confiscated and/or be fined.

U.S. duty rates for developed countries with Normal Trade Relations (NTR) are listed on the preceding page in Table 16.1. (Jewelry and gems from developing GSP countries are usually duty-free). Also listed are rates for countries without normal trade relations (non-NTR). Keep in mind that duty rates and country classifications are always subject to change, so these tariffs may be out of date when you read them.

In brief, jewelry bought in Canada, Mexico, Israel and developing countries is usually duty free when brought into the United States. Loose gemstones and pearls from any country with normal trade relations status are also in most cases duty free. If you import loose gems, customs will charge a merchandise processing fee of probably 0.21%.

For more specific information, contact your nearest customs office, which is normally at an international airport or seaport. You can find their addresses and phone numbers by going to
www.customs.treasgov/location/service1.htm
and clicking on the desired port of entry. Direct information from customs is more reliable than what you may hear from salespeople abroad. Some will tell you anything to get you to buy.

Tips on Avoiding Hassles with Customs

♦ **Keep a record of your purchases as you buy them.** It's easy to forget what you buy and how much you pay for it. Get receipts whenever possible and keep them in a safe place. For large purchases, it's a good idea to get duplicate receipts that you keep in separate places.

The night before you return home, go through your luggage and make sure all your purchases are written down. No matter how honest you are, you could be accused of smuggling if you forget something you bought.

♦ **If you travel with jewelry from home, take along a photocopy of the purchase receipt(s) or appraisal(s)**. When you return home, it's your responsibility to prove to customs that you didn't buy it abroad. Jewelry can't be registered with customs, except for certain watches. If you don't have receipts or appraisals, photograph the jewelry piece(s) next to something found only in your country, such as your car license plate. It's best, however, not to travel with expensive jewelry or watches.

By the way, customs officials are quite adept at using a loupe to determine if a watch you're wearing is new or not.

♦ **Register expensive items with serial numbers** such as cameras and laptop computers before you depart from your home country. This can be done at the airport.

♦ **Check the customs regulations** for your own country and for the countries you'll be passing through before your trip.

♦ When traveling through or to another country, **review in your mind beforehand where you're staying or who you're staying with.** This is a common question asked along borders such as the Canadian-American border, but it's easy to forget the answer. If you don't come up with an immediate response, expect a thorough search of your belongings.

♦ **If you plan to buy antiques, find out in advance what documentation and proof you'll need**. You may, for example, need an export certificate. To be duty free, antiques usually must be at least 100 years old. Regulations can vary from one country to another. Customs has a right to dispute any certificate you present.

♦ Most importantly, **tell the truth**.

Web Sites for Customs Regulations:

You can now find the customs regulations of most countries on the internet. The **World Customs Organization** (l'Organisation Mondiale des Douanes) provides information on customs agencies throughout the world. Its website address is

www.wcoomd.org/frmpublic.htm

and it has links to the customs websites of individual nations. You can reach these websites faster if you have their address. Listed below are countries which offer customs websites in English. Asian countries typically have bilingual websites.

Australia	www.customs.gov.au
Canada	www.ccra-adrc.gc.ca
China	www.customs.gov.cn
Cuba	www.aduana.islagrande.com
Dubai, United Arab Emirates	www.dxbcustoms.gov.ae
Fiji	www.fijicustoms.org.fj
Hong Kong	www.info.gov.hk/customs
Indonesia	www.beacukai.go.id
Iceland	www.tollur.is/english/customs.html
Ireland	www.revenue.ie
Japan	www.mof.go.jp/ ~ customs/conte-e.htm
Korea	www.customs.go.kr
Malaysia	www.customs.gov.my/
New Zealand	www.customs.govt.nz
Pakistan	www.cbr.gov.pk
Singapore	www.gov.sg/customs
Thailand	www.customs.go.th
United Kingdom	www.hmce.gov.uk
USA	www.customs.gov or
	www.customs.ustreas.gov

You can get customs information on countries not listed above through the www.wcoomd.org/frmpublic.htm website.

17

Finding a Good Buy

L ydia was touring South America. She hoped to buy an emerald as a souvenir while she was there because it was her birthstone. Before leaving on her trip, she read the *Ruby, Sapphire & Emerald Buying Guide* and the *Gem & Jewelry Pocket Guide*.

In order to determine if the salespeople were knowledgeable, Lydia would pick out an emerald and ask them to tell her something about its quality. Then she'd ask if it was treated or not. Most salespeople just said it was a great stone and then tried to evade her questions by changing the subject. One seller even started quoting poetry. Another said his emerald had a mysterious garden which added to its beauty. Many denied their emeralds were treated.

Finally, on her last day in South America, Lydia found a store manager in Brazil who was candid and able to evaluate emerald quality. His name was Antonio. He told her that the emerald she chose was average quality. Then he placed it next to a higher and lower quality emerald and pointed out some differences in color, clarity, transparency and cut. Unlike other sellers, he didn't mind having her examine the stones with a loupe. In addition, he didn't try to hide the fact that they were treated.

Lydia asked if he had any better emeralds, so he went to the safe and brought her two. She fell in love with one that was $16,000. It looked good in any type of light. Antonio showed her an AGL lab report of the stone which identified it as a natural Colombian emerald with an overall rating of excellent–very good. The degree of the oil type filler treatment was described as faint. Then he told Lydia he'd deduct three hundred dollars from the price so she could have the stone and report rechecked when she got back home.

Antonio's openness and knowledge made Lydia feel comfortable, so she went ahead and bought the emerald with a credit card. Antonio gave her a detailed receipt which stated in writing there was a 100% money back guarantee on the stone. Antonio's store had an office in the United States where she could return the stone if it turned out to be overpriced or misrepresented.

When Lydia returned to the United States, she immediately had the emerald appraised and then had it rechecked by AGL. The appraiser told her she got good value for her money and AGL confirmed that the stone and everything on their report matched. Afterwards, Lydia had the emerald mounted in a pendant. She was delighted with the results and with the fact that she had an ideal souvenir of a wonderful trip to South America.

Kinsey was in a Tahitian jewelry store looking through a bowl of black pearls. Before coming to Tahiti on holiday, she had read the *Pearl Buying Guide* and the *Gem & Jewelry Pocket Guide*. The salesman in the store told her that she could have any of the pearls in the bowl for the equivalent of $140. Kinsey first picked out the ones with the best luster. Then she eliminated those that had no overtone colors. Finally, with the help of the salesman, she selected a fairly large, tear-drop-shaped, greenish-gray pearl with purplish highlights. One side of the pearl, however, was badly flawed. But Kinsey planned to wear it as a pendant, so she knew the flaws wouldn't show.

On the flight back home, Kinsey sketched a design for the pendant and then later had her jeweler make it. He told her he could never have found a black pearl as attractive as hers for such a low price. When the pendant was finished, Kinsey tried it on. She was pleased with how it looked. But she was even more pleased that she now owns a unique souvenir of Tahiti which she helped create.

Buying gems turned out to be a positive experience for Lydia and Kinsey. This was largely because they took the time to learn about emeralds and pearls beforehand and they dealt with a competent salesperson. Listed on the next page are some guidelines that can help you become a smart buyer too.

◆ **Ask the salesperson to discuss the quality of the gems or jewelry** you're looking at. Competent salespeople will be able to point out specifics about the color, clarity, cut and craftsmanship. The more you spend, the more important it is to deal with qualified salespeople who can give you accurate advice.

◆ Before buying gems and jewelry, **look at a range of qualities and types.** This will give you a basis for comparison.

◆ **View gems(s) under different types of light**—fluorescent, incandescent (light bulbs), and daylight near a window. The color of gems can look different under various lights.

◆ **Examine gemstones under magnification** as well as with the unaided eye. Jewelers do this; so should you. Magnification will also help you evaluate jewelry craftsmanship.

◆ **Ask what kind of treatments the gemstone(s) has undergone.** The responses you receive will help you determine the value of the stone, the care requirements, and the competence and integrity of the salesperson.

◆ **Pay close attention to the quality of the cut**. Colored stones sold in many under-developed countries tend to have exceptionally large "windows" which allow you to see through them like glass.

◆ **Compare the per-carat prices of stones rather than their total cost.** Otherwise it will be difficult for you to make accurate comparisons. At the wholesale level, gems are priced according to per-carat cost.

◆ **Remember that there's no standardized system for grading colored gemstones.** As a consequence, grades have no meaning other than what the seller or grader assigns to them. This is another reason why you should look at stones yourself and learn to evaluate quality.

◆ **Note if the salesperson is willing to tell you the bad points about their merchandise along with the good ones.** It's impossible for everything in a jewelry showcase to be wonderful and perfect. Salespeople who care about their customers give them candid, objective information.

♦ **If possible, avoid closed-back settings** (those which completely cover the bottom of the stone and allow no light to shine through). They're frequently an indication that something is being hidden or that a stone is fake.

♦ **Have salespeople put their verbal claims in writing on the receipt.** For example, if they tell you a gem is untreated, they should be willing to state this on the receipt.

♦ **When buying very expensive items abroad, make sure that you can return the merchandise** if necessary. Get a written 100% money-back guarantee. If the item turns out to be misrepresented, an exchange will not be a convenient option.

Find out in advance if there's a way of insuring the merchandise when returning it. To most developing countries, you wouldn't be able to get, for example, $16,000 worth of insurance from the U.S. Post Office. **If there's no way for you to safely return expensive merchandise, don't buy it.** Find something of lesser value or else buy it at home where you have more consumer protection and more recourse. Gems are an international commodity, so you can find good buys on them in your home country too.

Shopping for gems and jewelry should be fun. There is no fun, though, in worrying about being deceived or in buying a stone that turns out to be a poor choice. Reread this book and follow the guidelines. Talk to jewelry professionals, look at gems whenever possible and read other literature. If you do, you'll not only be able to find good buys, you'll appreciate jewelry more and you'll have a great time shopping.

Suppliers of Gems & Jewelry for Photos

Cover photo: Rings from Cynthia Renée Co., Fallbrook, CA

Inside front cover photos:
Pearl brooch from A & Z Pearls, Los Angeles, CA
Ruby from Henry Ho, President Asian Institute of Gemological
Sciences (AIGS), Bangkok, Thailand

Inside back cover photos:
Bow Brooch from Barbara Berk Designs, Foster City, CA
Rings from Cynthia Renée Co., Fallbrook, CA

Half title page: Pendant from Barbara Berk, Foster City, CA

Title page: Pearls from King's Ransom, Sausalito, CA

Chapter 1
Figs. 1.2 & 1.4: Overland Gems, Los Angeles, CA
Figs. 1.6 & 1.7: Carrie G Fine Gems, Los Angeles, CA
Figs. 1.8 & 1.9: Josam Diamond Trading Corp.
Fig. 1.10: Port Royal Antique Jewelry, Naples, FL

Chapter 2
Figs. 2.1 &.2.2: American Gemological Laboratories, New York
Figs. 2.3 & 2.4: Josam Diamond Trading Corp., Los Angeles
Fig. 2.6: Fred Mouawad, Bangkok, Thailand

Chapter 3
Fig. 3.1: Varna Platinum, Los Angeles, CA

Chapter 4
Figs. 4.1 & 4.2: Overland Gems, Los Angeles, CA
Fig. 4.3: Andrew Sarosi, Los Angeles, CA
Fig. 4.5: Neshama, Los Angeles, CA
Fig. 4.6: Mark Gronlund, Enterprise, FL

Fig. 4.7: Barbara Berk Designs, Foster City, CA
Fig. 4.8: Glenn Lehrer Designs, Larkspur, CA
Fig. 4.10 & 4.11: American Gemological Laboratories, NY, NY
Fig. 4.12: Extreme Gioielli, Valenza, Italy
Fig. 4.13: Cynthia Renée Co., Fallbrook, CA
Fig. 4.14: Linda Quinn, Strafford, Missouri
Fig. 4.16: Mason-Kay, Inc., Denver, CO
Fig. 4.17: Richard Kimball, Denver, CO
Fig. 4.18: Overland Gems, Los Angeles, CA
Fig. 4.21: Timeless Gem Designs, Los Angeles, CA
Fig. 4.22: Carrie G Fine Gemstones, Los Angeles, CA
Fig. 4.23: Robert Shapiro, Madison, Wisconsin
Figs. 4.24 & 4.25: Neshama, Los Angeles, CA
Fig. 4.26: Port Royal Antique Jewelry, Naples, FL
Fig. 4.27: Cynthia Renée Co., Fallbrook, CA
Fig. 4.28: Asian Institute of Gemological Sciences, Bangkok
Fig. 4.29: Fred Mouawad, Bangkok, Thailand
Fig. 4.30: Carrie G and Andrew Sarosi, Los Angeles, CA
Fig. 4.31: Cynthia Renée Co., Fallbrook, CA
Fig. 4.32: Gary Dulac Goldsmith, Inc., Vero Beach, FL
Fig. 4.33: Carrie G Fine Gems, Los Angeles, CA
Fig. 4.34: Overland Gems, Los Angeles, CA
Fig. 4.35: Murphy Design, Minneapolis, MN
Fig. 4.36: Cynthia Renée Co., Fallbrook, CA
Fig. 4.37: Linda Quinn, Strafford, Missouri
Fig. 4.38: Extreme Gioielli, Valenza, Italy
Fig. 4.39: Neshama, Los Angeles, CA
Fig. 4.40: The Roxx Limited, Baltimore, MD
Fig. 4.41: Overland Gems, Los Angeles, CA

Chapter 5
Figs. 5.1 & 5.2 & 5.7: Joe Landau, Los Angeles, CA
Figs. 5.8–5.13: Josam Diamond Trading Corp., Los Angeles, CA
Fig. 5.14: Harry Winston, Inc., New York, NY

Chapter 6
Figs. 6.1–6.5: King Plutarco, Los Angeles, CA
Figs. 6.6 & 6.7: A & Z Pearls, Los Angeles, CA
Fig. 6.8: King's Ransom, Sausalito, CA
Fig. 6.9: Divina Pearls (formerly Tesoro Pearls), Santa Monica, CA

Chapter 7
Fig. 7.1: Barbara Berk Designs, Foster City, CA
Fig. 7.2: Siegfried Becker, White Plains, NY and Pforzheim, Germany
Fig. 7.3: Varna Platinum, Los Angeles, CA

Chapter 8
Fig. 8.2: Gregory Mikaelian and Peggy Croft, Los Angeles, CA
Fig. 8.7: Varna Platinum, Los Angeles, CA

Chapter 9
Fig. 9.1: King's Ransom, Sausalito, CA
Fig. 9.2: Mason-Kay, Inc., Denver, CO
Fig. 9.5: Carrie G Fine Gems, Los Angeles, CA
Fig. 9.7: Barbara Berk, Foster City, CA
Fig. 9.9: Fred Mouawad, Bangkok, Thailand
Fig. 9.10: Danny & Ronny Levy Fine Gems, Los Angeles, CA

Identification Tables and Birthstones

Moh's Hardness of untreated gems mentioned in this book (hardness is a material's resistance to scratching and abrasions):

Diamond	10	Feldspars	6½–7
Ruby	9	Jadeite	6½–7
Sapphire	9	Jasper	6½–7
Chrysoberyl	8½	Kunzite	6½–7
Spinel	8	Peridot	6½–7
Topaz	8	Tanzanite	6½–7
Aquamarine	7½–8	Moonstone	6–6½
Beryl	7½–8	Nephrite	6–6½
Emerald	7½–8	Opal	5½–6½
Iolite	7–7½	Lapis Lazuli	5–6
Tourmaline	7–7½	Turquoise	5–6
Zircon	7–7½	Malachite	3½–4
Amethyst	7	Coral	3–4
Quartz	7	Pearl	2½–4½
Garnet	6½–7½	Ivory	2½
Chalcedony	6½–7	Amber	2–2½

Refractive Index (R.I.—the degree to which light is bent as it passes through the stone. As a general rule, the higher the R.I., the greater the potential brilliance of the stone and the harder it is to see through the stone when it's faceted.)

Diamond	2.417	Turquoise	1.65–1.61
Zircon	1.92–1.81	Tourmaline	1.64–1.62
Garnet	1.87–1.72	Topaz	1.63–1.61
Ruby/Sapphire	1.77–1.76	Nephrite	1.63–1.61
Chrysoberyl	1.76–1.75	Beryl (emerald)	1.58–1.57
Spinel	1.72	Quartz (amethyst)	1.55–1.54
Tanzanite	1.70–1.69	Iolite	1.54–1.53
Peridot	1.69–1.65	Moonstone	1.54–1.52
Pearl	1.69–1.53	Amber	1.54
Jadeite	1.68–1.66	Chalcedony	1.54–1.53
Kunzite	1.67–1.66	Opal	1.44–1.46

Specific Gravity (S.G.—the ratio of a material's weight to the weight of an equal volume of water at 4°C; indicates how dense and heavy a material is); these are general S.G. values; the exact S.G. varies depending on the variety and locality.

Platinum	21.4	Kunzite	3.18
Pure gold	19.3	Tourmaline	3.06
Silver	10.6	Nephrite	2.95
Copper	8.9	Turquoise	2.76
Zircon	4.7–4.0	Lapis Lazuli	2.75
Garnet	4.2–3.5	Beryl	2.72
Ruby/Sapphire	4.0	Pearl	2.70
Malachite	3.3–4.1	Quartz	2.66
Chrysoberyl	3.7	Coral	2.65
Spinel	3.6	Iolite	2.61
Topaz	3.53	Chalcedony	2.60
Diamond	3.52	Moonstone	2.56
Peridot	3.34	Opal	2.15
Jadeite	3.34	Ivory	1.7–2.0
Tanzanite	3.35	Amber	1.08

The information in the preceding tables is from *Gems* by Robert Webster, *Gemstones of the World* by Robert Schumann and *Handbook of Gem Identification* by Richard T. Liddicoat, Jr.

Birthstones established in 1912 by the American National Retail Jewelers' Association:

January	Garnet
February	Amethyst
March	Bloodstone or aquamarine
April	Diamond
May	Emerald
June	Pearl or moonstone
July	Ruby
August	Peridot or sardonyx
September	Sapphire
October	Opal or tourmaline
November	Topaz
December	Turquoise or lapis lazuli

Bibliography

Books and Booklets

AGTA, *1997-98 Source Directory* & Gemstone Enhancement Information Chart

Ahrens, Joan & Malloy, Ruth. *Hong Kong Gems & Jewelry*. Hong Kong: Delt. Dragon, 1986.

Arem, Joel. *Color Encyclopedia of Gemstones*. New York: Chapman & Hall

Arem, Joel. *Gems & Jewelry*. New York: Bantam, 1986.

Bauer, Dr. Max. *Precious Stones*. Rutland, Vermont & Tokyo: Charles E Tuttle, 1969.

Beesley, C. R. *Gemstone Training Manual*. American Gem Laboratories.

Bingham, Anne. Buying Jewelry. New York: McGraw Hill, 1989.

Ciprani, Curzio & Borelli, Alessandro. *Simon & Schuster's Guide to Gems and Precious Stones*. New York: Simon and Schuster, 1986.

Farrington, Oliver Cummings. *Gems and Gem Minerals*. Chicago: A. W. Mum ford, 1903.

Federman, David & Hammid, Tino. *Consumer Guide to Colored Gemstones* Shawnee Mission, Modern Jeweler, 1989.

Gemological Institute of America. *Gem Reference Guide*. Santa Monica, CA GIA, 1988.

Geolat, Patti, Van Northrup, C., Federman, David. *The Professional's Guide to Jewelry Insurance Appraising*. Lincolnshire, IL: Vance Publishing Corporation, 1994.

Gubelin, Eduard J. & Koivula, John I. *Photoatlas of Inclusions in Gemstones*. Zurich: ABC Edition, 1986.

Hall, Cally. *Gemstones*. New York: Dorling Kindersley, 1994.

Hanneman, W. Wm. *Naming Gem Garnets*. Poulsbo, WA: Hanneman Gemological Instruments, 2000.

Hughes, Richard W. *Ruby & Sapphire*, Boulder, CO: RWH Publishing, 1997.

Jewelers of America. *The Gemstone Enhancement Manual*. New York: Jewelers of America, 1990.

eller, Peter. *Gemstones of East Africa*. Phoenix: Geoscience Press Inc., 1992.

unz, George & Stephenson, Charles. *The Book of the Pearl*. New York: Century Co., 1908.

iddicoat, Richard T. *Handbook of Gem Identification*. Santa Monica, CA: GIA, 1981.

Marcum, David. *Fine Gems and Jewelry*. Homewood: Dow Jones-Irwin, 1986.

McCreight, Tim. *The Complete Metalsmith: An Illustrated Handbook*. Worcester, MA: Davis Publications, 1991.

Nassau, Kurt. *Gems Made by Man*. Santa Monica, CA: GIA, 1980.

Nassau, Kurt. *Gemstone Enhancement*, Second Edition. London: Butterworths, 1994.

Newman, Renée. *Diamond Ring Buying Guide: Fifth Edition*. Los Angeles: International Jewelry Publications, 1999.

Newman, Renée. *Emerald & Tanzanite Buying Guide* LA: I.J.P. 1996.

Newman, Renée. *Gemstone Buying Guide*. Los Angeles: International Jewelry Publications, 1998.

Newman, Renée. *Gold & Platinum Jewelry Buying Guide: How to Judge, Buy, Test & Care for It*. LA: International Jewelry Publications, 2000.

Newman, Renée. *Pearl Buying Guide: Third Edition*. Los Angeles: International Jewelry Publications, 1999.

Newman, Renée. *Ruby & Sapphire Buying Guide*. LA: I.J.P. 1994.

Newman, Renée. *Ruby, Sapphire & Emerald Buying Guide: How to evaluate, identify, select & care for these gemstones*. Los Angeles: International Jewelry Publications, 2000.

O'Donoghue, Michael. *Identifying Man-made Gems*. London: N.A.G. Press, 1983.

O'Donoghue, Michael. *Synthetic, Imitation & Treated Gemstones*. Oxford: Butterworth-Heinemann, 1997.

Pagel-Theisen, Verena. *Diamond Grading ABC*. New York: Rubin & Son, 1986.

Read, Peter G. *Gemmology*. Oxford: Butterworth-Heineman, 1996.

Revere, Alan, *Professional Goldsmithing*. New York: Van Nostrand Reinhold, 1991.

Roskin, Gary. *Photo Masters For Diamond Grading*. Northbrook, IL: Gemworld International, 1994.

Rubin, Howard & Levine. Gail, GemDialogue Color Tool Box. Rego Park, NY, GemDialogue Systems, Inc., 1997.

Rubin, Howard. *Grading & Pricing with GemDialogue*. NY: GemDialogue Marketing Co., 1986.

Schumann, Walter. *Gemstones of the World: Revised & Expanded Edition*. New York: Sterling, 1997.

Sinkankas, John. *Emerald and other Beryls*. Prescott, AZ: Geoscience Press,

SSEF Swiss Gemmological Institute. *Standards & Applications for Diamond Report,, Gemstone Report, Test Report*..Basel: SSEF Swiss Gemmological Institute, 1998.

Suwa, Yasukazu. *Gemstones Quality & Value* (English Edition). GIA and Suwa & Son, Inc., 1994.

Suwa, Yasukazu. *Gemstones Quality & Value: Volume 2*. Tokyo: Sekai Bunka Publishing, Inc., 1997.

Voillot, Patrick. *Diamond & Precious Stones*. New York: Abrams, 1998.

Webster, Robert. *Gems*. London: Butterworths, 1990

White, John S. *The Smithsonian Treasury Minerals and Gems*. Washington D.C Smithsonian Institution Press, 1991.

Woodward, Christine & Harding, Roger. *Gemstones*. New York: Sterling, 1988

Periodicals

AJM, American Jewelry Manufacturer. Providence, RI.

Anglic Gemcuuter. POB 826, Beavercreek, OR. 97004.

Auction Market Resource for Gems & Jewelry. P. O. Box 7683 Rego Park NY. 11374.

Australian Gemmologist. Brisbane: Gemmological Association of Australia

Canadian Gemmologist. Toronto: Canadian Gemmological Association.

Colored Stone. Devon, PA: Lapidary Journal Inc.

GAA Market Monitor Precious Gem Appraisal/Buying Guide. Pittsburgh, PA.

Gemkey Magazine. Bangkok, Thailand: Gemkey Co., Ltd.

Gem & Jewellery News. London. Gemmological Association and Gem Testing Laboratory of Great Britain.

Gems and Gemology. Santa Monica, CA: Gemological Institute of America.

Gemstone Price Reports. Brussels: Ubige S.P.R.L.

The Guide. Northbrook Intl. Inc: Gemworld International, Inc.

Lapidary Journal. Devon, PA: Lapidary Journal Inc.

Jewelers Circular Keystone. Radnor, PA: Chilton Publishing Co.

Jewelers' Quarterly Magazine. Sonoma, CA.

Journal of Gemmology, London: Gemmological Association and Gem Testing Laboratory of Great Britain.

Modern Jeweler. Lincolnshire, IL: Vance Publishing Inc.

National Jeweler. New York: Gralla Publications.

Professional Jeweler. Philadelphia: Bond Communications.

Palmieri's Auction/FMV Monitor. Pittsburgh, PA: GAA

Index

Order Form

TITLE	Price Each	Quantity	Total
Gem & Jewelry Pocket Guide	$ 11.95		
Pearl Buying Guide	$ 19.95		
Gemstone Buying Guide	$ 19.95		
Ruby, Sapphire & Emerald Buying Guide	$ 19.95		
Gold & Platinum Jewelry B. G.	$ 19.95		
Diamond Ring Buying Guide 5th edition, available June 2001	$ 17.95		
		BOOK TOTAL:	
SALES TAX for California residents only (book total x $.0825)			
SHIPPING: USA: first book $1.75, each additional copy $.75 Foreign surface mail: first book $3.00; ea. addl. $1.50 Canada & Mexico - airmail: $5.00 per book All other foreign destinations airmail: first book $11.00, ea. addl. $6.00			
Total amount with tax (if applicable) and shipping (Pay foreign orders with an international money order or a check drawn on a U.S. bank.) **TOTAL:**			

Mail check or money order in U.S. funds

To: Intl. Jewelry Publications
P.O. Box 13384
Los Angeles, CA 90013-0384
USA

OTHER PUBLICATIONS BY RENEE NEWMAN

Diamond Ring Buying Guide

"**By far the best diamond book ever made...**Warns you of sca▌ other books ignore or gloss over...Topics covered include diamo▌ terms, the 4C's, chart of actual sizes in carats, detailed mechanic▌ drawings, stunning color photos of diamond cuts and shapes, diamo▌ colors, treated diamonds, good and bad cuts. Then there are pho▌ to help you tell the difference between fake and real, fracture fil▌ synthetic diamonds...Buying tips, custom ring tips, diamond cleanir▌ storage, preventing diamond switching, and lots more. This truly▌ a diamond bible."

Jeff Ostroff, *BridalTips.com*

140 p., 109 photos, 7" X 9", ISBN 0-929975-24-3, $14.95 U▌
New 6th edition with more photos available June 2001 for $17.9▌

Gemstone Buying Guide

"**A quality Buying Guide** that is recommended for purchase▌ consumers, gemmologists and students of gemmology—irrespecti▌ of their standard of knowledge of gemmology. The information▌ comprehensive, factual, and well presented. Particularly notewort▌ in this book are the 189 quality colour photographs that have be▌ carefully chosen to illustrate the text."

Australian Gemmologist

"**Praiseworthy**, a beautiful gem-pictorial reference and a help▌ everyone in viewing colored stones as a gemologist or gem deal▌ would...One of the finest collections of gem photographs I've ev▌ seen...If you see the book, you will probably purchase it on t▌ spot."

Anglic Gemcutter

"**Beautifully produced**...With colour on almost every opening, fe▌ could resist this book whether or not they were in the gem a▌ jewellery trade. The book should be on the counter or by the bedsi▌ (or both)."

Journal of Gemmology

152 p., 189 photos, 7" X 9", ISBN 0-929975-25-1, $19.95 US▌

Ruby, Sapphire & Emerald Buying Guide
How to Evaluate, Identify, Select & Care for these Gemstones

"The best produced book on gemstones I have yet seen in this price range (how is it done?). This is the book for anyone who buys, sells or studies gemstones. This style of book (and similar ones by the same author) is the only one I know which introduces actual trade conditions and successfully combines a good deal of gemmology with gem...**Buy it, read it, keep it**."

Michael O'Donoghue, *Journal of Gemmology*

"**Solid, informative and comprehensive**...dissects each aspect of ruby and sapphire value in detail...a wealth of grading information...a definite thumbs-up. There is something here for everyone."

C. R. Beesley, President, American Gemological Laboratories.

164 p., 175 photos, 7" by 9", ISBN 0-929975-28-6, $19.95 US

Gold & Platinum Jewelry Buying Guide
How to Judge, Buy, Test & Care for It

"Enjoyable reading...profusely illustrated with color photographs showing not only the beauty of finished jewelry but close-ups and magnification of details such as finish, settings, flaws and fakes.. sophisticated enough for professionals to use...highly recommended... **Newman's guides are the ones to take along when shopping.**"

Library Journal

156 p., 194 photos, 6 3/4" by 9", ISBN 0-929975-29-4, $19.95 US

Pearl Buying Guide

"**If you're thinking of investing in pearls, invest $20 first in the *Pearl Buying Guide***...Even if you already own pearls, this book has good tips on care and great ideas on different ways to wear pearls."

San Jose Mercury News

"**...A gem-dandy guide to picking right-price pearls**."

Boston Herald

150 p., 151 photos, 7" by 9", ISBN 0-929975-27-8, $19.95

Order Form

TITLE	Price Each	Quantity	Total
Gem & Jewelry Pocket Guide	$ 11.95		
Pearl Buying Guide	$ 19.95		
Gemstone Buying Guide	$ 19.95		
Ruby, Sapphire & Emerald Buying Guide	$ 19.95		
Gold & Platinum Jewelry B. G.	$ 19.95		
Diamond Ring Buying Guide 6th edition, available June 2001	$ 17.95		
		BOOK TOTAL:	
SALES TAX for California residents only (book total x $.0825)			
SHIPPING: USA: first book $1.75, each additional copy $.75 Foreign surface mail: first book $3.00; ea. addl. $1.50 Canada & Mexico - airmail: $5.00 per book All other foreign destinations airmail: first book $11.00, ea. addl. $6.00			
Total amount with tax (if applicable) and shipping (Pay foreign orders with an international money order or a check drawn on a U.S. bank.) **TOTAL:**